A Feminist Companion to Social Psychology

Series: Feminist Companions to Psychology Series
Series Editors: Sarah Riley, Rose Cadevila, & Hannah Frith

A Feminist Companion to Social Psychology

Madeleine Pownall and
Wendy Stainton Rogers

Mc Graw Hill

Open University Press

Open University Press
McGraw Hill
8th Floor, 338 Euston Road
London
England
NW1 3BH

email: enquiries@openup.co.uk
world wide web: www.openup.co.uk

First edition published 2021

A catalogue record of this book is available from the British Library

ISBN-13: 9780335250752
ISBN-10: 0335250750
eISBN: 9780335250769

Library of Congress Cataloging-in-Publication Data
CIP data applied for

Typeset by Transforma Pvt. Ltd., Chennai, India

Praise page

This engaging, funny, but also deeply serious book captivated and delighted me! It provides the companion I would have loved to have had access to in my psychology undergraduate degree – a feminist friend to help you navigate and find your place in – or against – the (White) malestream of the discipline. Featuring scholarship and activism from around the globe, and across the decades, Madeleine Pownall and Wendy Stainton Rogers' book pings with the vibrancy and creativity of feminist critique. With this companion, they have made feminist inspiration, analysis, and activism easily accessible to everyone studying social psychology!

Virginia Braun, Professor of Psychology, The University of Auckland, New Zealand

A big thank you to Madeleine Pownall and Wendy Stainton-Rogers for showcasing the impressive contributions that feminist scholars have made to the psychological study of social life. In lucid and lively prose, the Feminist Companion ushers readers through a compendium of scholarship that spans the Anglophone world and crosses into several disciplines. Beyond bare "findings," Pownall and Stainton Rogers describe the diverse standpoints, methodological critiques and innovations, epistemological debates, activist projects, and ethical commitments of feminist psychologists. The Feminist Companion was written for undergraduate readers, but it holds much wisdom for us all.

Jeanne Marecek, Swarthmore College, Swarthmore, Pennsylvania, USA

Extremely lively and super-smart, this Feminist Companion is indeed the friend you want to sit beside in every social psychology class. Pownall and Stainton Rogers provide a fresh, feisty, up-to-the moment feminist take on the dynamic field that is social psychology. Students will come away with practical skills and critical insights that will indelibly influence how they see this field, and indeed all of psychology.

Alexandra Rutherford, Professor, Historical, Theoretical and Critical Studies of Psychology, York University, Canada

Dedication

This book is dedicated to the memory of the amazing and sublime Professor Marcia Worrell, a woman of many excellent virtues and a true feminist in so many ways. Her legacy is broad and deep, her kindness and concern has touched so many lives, and she brought much joy to this world. We miss you Marce, especially your laugh and your wicked sense of fun

Contents

Series Preface

About the *Feminist Companion* Series

Series Editors: Sarah Riley, Rose Capdevila and Hannah Frith

As Series Editors we can each remember pivotal moments during our under-graduate psychology studies when we were exposed to feminist research and theorising. These moments have shaped our own identities as feminists, our approach to teaching, learning and research in psychology, and our engagements with psychology as a discipline. There are some fantastic feminist psychology lecturers and mentors. For those of us who are fortunate to be taught by them, these are experiences that we never forget.

Hannah

For me, this came in the form of my second-year undergraduate module on research methods in psychology. On the first day of this module, in bounced my teacher (Celia Kitzinger) brimming with energy and enthusiasm, and bursting with exciting ideas about research. I was brought up short by a double whammy of learning about qualitative research for the first time and realising (with some surprise) that research might involve talking with, learning from, and respectfully listening to people. Hearing the voices of women, talking about issues important to women's lives for the first time, lit a fire in me.

Rose

Reading feminist literature was an integral part of my undergraduate degree in politics. There were loads of stats and stories that could tell you the world wasn't fair, no convincing needed. However, the real revelation came when I attended a departmental talk shortly after starting my PhD in Psychology. Usually these talks revolved around experiments, controlling variables and producing statistical analyses. However, the speaker that week (Christine Griffin) didn't do this. She talked about her research with young, working class women; how they were constructed – both inside and outside of academia – as 'troubled' when they behaved in certain ways, and how this was used to manage them. The speaker described how, by using qualitative methods, researchers could explore the world in ways that valued experience and relationships, rather than converting them into variables to be measured and controlled. I had never thought of things in that way, and it opened up a whole new approach to making sense of world. Much reading followed.

Sarah

My story is slightly different. I had some great teachers and supervisors at undergraduate level, but none were explicitly feminist, other than a course on gender which was cancelled the year I could have done it while the lecturer was on sabbatical. In my research project though, I was supported to do feminist experimental research, but my greatest feminist education came from my friends Emma and Terry, who were studying Philosophy, Women's Studies and Russian Studies, and who taught me the art of thinking, arguing and drinking. There were also important books that gave me language for understanding my world, it felt like they explained what I already knew, but hadn't had the words to describe.

In our stories, we offer a range of experiences. Face-to-face with visionary feminist psychologists or peer taught – we had people with us on our feminist journey. But not everybody does. Although feminist research and theorising has grown enormously over the many years since we were undergraduates (continuing a trend which began way before then), it remains marginalised in most undergraduate curricula and teachers can be unsure about how to integrate feminism into their classes. At the same time, feminist activism outside of academia is flourishing; Everyday Sexism, SlutWalks, #MeToo, Everyone's Invited, and the Million Women March are just a few examples. Curricula which fail to include feminist scholarship risks failing to engage students who want to see the psychology they study reflecting what is important in their lives.

The *Feminist Companions to Psychology* series was born out of a desire to address these gaps. It draws on the historic strengths of Open University Press of taking complex concepts and presenting them in a clear and accessible way, and aims to provide resources to support staff who are looking to incorporate the latest feminist thinking into their existing modules.

We wanted to develop short, snappy, pedagogically informed books which would sit alongside – as well as complement, complicate, and contest – psychology textbooks and courses. We wanted to support teachers and mentors in psychology by providing short, accessible books which speak to the British Psychological Society's curriculum areas (starting with the core areas of social, cognitive, developmental, biological, personality & individual differences and research methods). We wanted to engage undergraduate psychologists in academic work which might speak to their values, their activism, or help them make sense of their experiences. We also think psychology undergraduates are missing out! Feminist psychology is a diverse, multifaceted field of work creating cutting edge, energising psychology that challenges all of us to think and act in new ways. It's important that we share it with the next generation of psychology students. This series is a celebration of the fun, fierce, fabulous and wonderful things that feminism has to offer to psychology.

About *A Feminist Companion to Social Psychology*

Series Editors: Sarah Riley, Rose Capdevila and Hannah Frith

In this highly engaging book, Madeleine and Wendy take you through a feminist tour de force of social psychology. They show how early feminist researchers pushed through the patriarchal "founding fathers" of psychology's viewpoint – where if women were considered at all it was in terms of measuring their inferiority – to reframe understandings of gender, women, femininity and inequality. Much of this involved creating a language to speak about these issues and developing approaches to understand the complexity of social interaction, social identities, power, representation and more. These developments are ongoing, with contemporary social psychology negotiating a range of challenges and exciting opportunities, including the replication crisis in experimental social psychology; challenges from critical black scholarship that have illuminated the need for an intersectional lens; and LGBTQIA+ scholarship and activism that invites us all to rethink gender and sexuality.

Engaging and accessible, Madeleine and Wendy examine classic and contemporary studies across social psychology research, exploring the kinds of questions psychologists ask about our social lives. Their feminist lens illuminates the deployment of power; intersectionality; diversity; social and communal lives; social justice; the interpretation of research methods; the values of respect, generosity, kindness and humility, and the worth of disruptive, critical feminist troublemaking. In so doing, they prepare the reader for the challenges involved in tackling the big questions of justice, power and agency. They do this by exploring a range of approaches to social psychology, including experimental and laboratory studies and social constructionist work that centres lived experience; throughout they consider the core questions that are asked within social psychology.

This book examines the core BPS curriculum in social psychology through a feminist lens, exploring a range of topics that are important to students, including, sexual harassment, casual sex, interactions in nightclubs, desirable and unwanted identities, and how to have equal relationships.

Introducing students to different epistemological approaches to research (positivist, phenomenological, social constructionist, to name but a few), they show how feminist research has used all of these approaches to challenge existing paradigms and generate new forms of knowledge. The book helps develop students' critical and analytical skills by encouraging a questioning approach to understanding social psychology research, and by offering alternative, feminist informed approaches – including inviting students to join the increasing band of feminist killjoys!

It is also a unique resource to support staff who are looking to incorporate the latest feminist thinking into their social psychology modules.

Welcome to *A Feminist Companion to Social Psychology*, an adventure in social justice thinking.

Acknowledgements

From Madeleine

Wendy Stainton Rogers has taught me more than I thought imaginable during the course of writing this Companion. Wendy has been a kind, supportive, dedicated co-author who has made me a better writer and a more thoughtful feminist.

I am a feminist primarily because of my mother, Gill Paxton. She brought me up with the now-infamous motto 'tits and teeth, girls!' (aka shoulders back, big smile), which I often think about when I'm in situations that make me want to run back to bed and hide (like when I'm asked if I'd like to write a feminist text-book with one of my heroes). My interest in feminist social psychology was later ignited by Patrick Hylton and Nathan Heflick at the University of Lincoln. They introduced me to the wonderful, messy world of social psychology. A few years later, once I had discovered POWES (the Psychology of Women and Equalities Section of the BPS), the jig was well and truly up. I was converted!

This book is the product of countless conversations over coffee, chats over a glass of wine at conferences, and excited WhatsApp messages. Therefore, I have a whole army of wonderful academics and friends who have inspired, challenged, and supported me over the course of writing this book. Thank you especially to Lucy Prodgers; Liz Travis; Crissie Harney; Anita Balcer-Whittle; Pam Birtill; Richard Harris; Mark Pownall; Eric, Flo, and Anna; Catherine Talbot; Olly Robertson; my Feminist Open Science Dream Team and my lovely PsyPAG family.

A special thank you to Paul Spillane for the weekly polygon sessions over FaceTime that saw me through weekends of 'working on the book'.

Finally, thank you to Hugh. This book was written during the lockdown of 2020–2021, which meant we spent every waking hour in each other's company. I have never known so much fun. Thank you for listening to me, wide-eyed and excited, whenever I talked about which bit of 'the book' I was working on that day. Thank you for interrupting my writing with impromptu dance parties. Thank you for regularly tapping me on my shoulder, grinning, and giving me a thumbs up as I spent hours on Zoom to Wendy. For every frosty walk around Beckett Park, for every Fika, and for every mug of coffee you brought me while I was writing. Thank you.

From Wendy

I too have learned so much from Madeleine. These days I am pretty weak, phys-ically and mentally, and her strength, positivity, amazing ICT skills, knowledge of the leading edge of social psychology, her kindness and sheer enthusiasm have lifted me up and sorted me out over and over again. I have also been supported in this venture within the POWES community, and over this last year they have made me a far better informed and more committed feminist. I really value and appreciate the way women work together so supportively and respectfully. I would like to mention Rose Capdevila, Michelle Fine, Catriona Macleod, and Bridgette Rickett for being especially supportive to me in my retirement. I, too, was inspired by my mother, who set her sights high for her three daughters. She taught us so much – about how to be outrageous rather than timid (by holding cherry-stone spitting competitions on the way home from shopping), and how to make ourselves heard and taken notice of. She insisted we all gained the qualifications to make ourselves economically independent, and expected us to excel at school – when our friends' mothers were just after 'a good marriage' and grandchildren.

I would also like to add my profound appreciation of the NHS. The skills and caregiving of so many of its staff have saved my life several times over and keep me alive now. During the pandemic they have been our heroes, and I thank them all for getting us through such a difficult year – and more. But so too have all the frontline workers who have kept me comfortable and fed. I would like to thank especially our neighbours, John and Lynne Sylvester, who promised to keep us safe and did all our shopping and posting, and sorted anything else we needed through the many months of shielding. And within all this, my lovely husband Robin Long has been the most wonderful medical carer. Nothing that I do would be possible without his care, or his wicked smile.

From both of us

We are lucky enough to have also been writing this Companion within a highly supportive feminist team at Open University Press. Thanks in particular go to our wonderful Editor, Clara Heathcock, a true inspiration to us both and an excellent woman to turn to when the going gets tough; and her trusty assistant, Beth Summers, whose cheerful willingness to do the 'little stuff' has smoothed many a troubled brow. Our Series Editors – Rose Capdevila, Hannah Frith, and Sara Riley – have provided thoughtful and sometimes provocative feedback that has benefitted the book enormously. In this context, writing this Companion has felt like going on a very exciting adventure, backed up by a fabulous team we knew we could trust. Thanks sisters, it's been fun!

Introduction: How to use this Companion

There are lots of different kinds of *Companion* books. A-level psychology Companions usually comprise really helpful 'beginner guides', which give basic and general advice about psychology as an academic subject, a list of its different topics and specialisms, advice about how to study it and, in particular, how to pass the exam. Bluntly, these kinds of Companions can often make psychology feel rather boring, as they generally present psychology content in a way that is fairly uncritical. They also tend to leave out the saucy bits of psychology's history (and present) and shy away from anything too wildly controversial.

At the other end of the spectrum, there are the much more advanced forms of *Companion* books, such as *The Routledge Companion to Philosophy of Psychology*. This particular Companion is an enormous doorstep of a book, made up of a series of 48 chapters commissioned by its editors, each of which is written by world experts on their area of world-class scholarship. These are mainly reference books like this providing a comprehensive coverage of a particular field. Libraries tend to buy them (although they're often pretty expensive), and they usually spend most of their lives hidden away on dusty shelves

Our Companion is like neither of these. We have written this Companion book to be a lot more friendly and (importantly) a lot more fun. As authors, we (Madeleine and Wendy) are two feminists, one in her twenties and the other in her seventies. We have had a fab time planning, plotting, and writing this Companion together. Throughout the following chapters, we'd like you to think of us as the somewhat cynical, slightly giggly friend who sits beside you when you're reading a paper, listening to a lecture, or engaging in a seminar, whispering things like: 'actually, there's another way of looking at that!', and, occasionally, hissing, 'that's a load of patriarchal rubbish!' We are your unofficial feminist friends who plan to take you on an incredible journey through selected parts of the social psychology undergraduate curriculum. Our mission is to show you the wonders of feminist invention, of feminists' cunning deconstruction of man-made language, the courage and determination of our founding mothers, and to shock you with tales of psychology's 'Horrible Histories' of sexual harassment (including in its experiments).

We invite you to join us in our circus of the patriarchal vanities: amazing acts of mansplaining and bropriation; the dreadfulness of compulsory heteronormativity and TERFing; and the critical, creative wonder that is feminist scholarship. This is not going to be a walk in the park, so brace yourself! But we have designed some rather cunning features to make your quest for a feminist nirvana just a bit easier:

Boxes

Throughout the Companion, you will come across information aside from the main text in boxes. These highlight particular 'key points' that are important to expanding your insight and understanding. They won't always be central to our core message but will provide you with additional nuggets of information that may be useful to you as you develop your feminist consciousness.

Activities

As we will remind you throughout the Companion, being a feminist is a 'practical endeavour'. It is not just about sitting around reading; it is also about *doing*. To reflect this, we have included some hands-on activities in each chapter. These are obviously optional – unless you have your own feminist harridan who will be keeping an eye on you and assessing your progress. But there is extensive evidence that your active participation in your learning makes it much more effective. We have tried to prevent them feeling like homework, and to make them interesting, creating emotional engagement as well as helping you to develop a 'feminist toolkit' for the future. Some of them are particularly useful to do in pairs or small groups (which we note throughout), and some are designed to be reflective exercises that you can do solo.

See and hear for yourself

As well as working through some guided activities, we also point you to examples where you can see feminist social psychology 'in action', often in 'the wild' (rather than just in journal articles and other books!). 'See and hear for yourself' exercises include links to online videos like TED-talks, interviews with some of feminist social psychology's most impressive and inspirational women, and ideas about film and TV which can show you feminism 'in action'. For example, hearing Carol Gilligan's account of her career, from being a lowly assistant to two of social psychology's founding figures to becoming herself one of its stars is, in our view, very moving and utterly inspirational.

Summaries

To help you to orientate your way around the book, we have included a summary box at the end of every section of the chapter, and an overall chapter summary for each. These are a useful way of calibrating your learning as you go along and can be helpful when it comes to revising what you've learnt at the end of the Companion.

Glossary

Feminist social psychology draws upon a rich and complex history of equality, psychology, social justice, and research. Therefore, sometimes we will use words and phrases that require a little more definition and explanation. To help guide us you through the Companion without interrupting ourselves, we have created a glossary of terms which you will find at the end of the book. Whenever you see a word that is both ***bold and italic***, you will find it in the Glossary.

Learning objectives

We will cover a lot of ground together over the next nine chapters! To help you to understand what it is that you should be getting from each chapter, we start each one with some clear learning objectives. These tell you about what the chapter will cover and how it relates to what you've learned so far.

Mapping this Companion against QAA and BPS curricula

This Companion is designed to accompany the British Psychological Society's (BPS) core undergraduate curriculum (2019), as informed by the QAA Subject Benchmark Statement for Psychology. Here, we provide a detailed breakdown of how the topics, theories, and debates covered in this Companion map onto the social psychology topics as outlined by the QAA (Table 1). We then examine how this Companion also maps onto the requirements of the 'Conceptual and Historical Issues in Psychology' area of the BPS curriculum. Finally, we end this section by identifying how the content in this Companion aligns broadly with the graduate skills that the BPS indicates is required for Graduate Basis for Chartership in psychology.

Table 1:   Mapping this Companion to the QAA topics in Social Psychology

Chapter	QAA topics *Section 3.3: Subject Benchmark Statement*	Description
Chapter 1: Introducing feminist social psychology	Social constructionism Culture	Chapter 1 introduces students to social constructionism, decolonisation of social psychology, and generally welcomes students to the world of feminist social psychology through this lens
Chapter 2: How (and why) is social psychology changing?	Group processes Intergroup relations Social cognition	This chapter covers some of the classic social psychology theories and studies, such as Sherif's Robbers Cave experiment, intergroup relations, and social cognition

Table 1:   (*Continued*)

Chapter	QAA topics *Section 3.3: Subject Benchmark Statement*	Description
Chapter 3: Gender, identity, and intersectionality	Self and identity Culture Social constructionism	This chapter explores the gendered aspect of identity, drawing upon social identity theory and demonstrating the complexity of identity
Chapter 4: Social psychology's horrible history	Self and identity Leadership Attitudes	This chapter looks at the history of social psychology, examining how attitudes towards women have led to gender inequality, whilst highlighting the work that has been done to correct this
Chapter 5: Prejudice, stereotyping, and objectification	Attitudes Social cognition Culture Self and identity	This chapter covers some of the core issues and debates in attitude and social cognition research, including implicit associations, Othering, and sexism
Chapter 6: Delusions of gender	Self and identity Attitudes Social constructionism	This chapter takes an explicitly social constructivist approach to sex differences, noting how findings from social psychological research can enforce negative attitudes and prejudice
Chapter 7: Communication and language	Social constructionism Intergroup relations Culture	This chapter introduces students to alternative approaches to studying communication, including qualitative techniques. It also examines cultural, societal, and social connotations of language use
Chapter 8: Roles and relationships	Close relationships Culture	This chapter critically assesses the social psychological literature on close relationships, including female friendships, and social roles, including mothering
Chapter 9: Looking forward to your fabulous feminist future	Social constructionism Leadership Culture	The final chapter encourages students to take what they have learned in the Companion forward, by applying their new-found knowledge and skills to addressing global and societal problems

Conceptual and historical issues in psychology

As well as the topics for Social Psychology, the BPS and QAA also include 'conceptual and historical issues in psychology' as one of the core components of a psychology undergraduate degree. This Companion is well aligned to this area of subject knowledge too.

Table 2: Mapping this Companion to BPS subject knowledge

BPS subject knowledge: Conceptual and historical issues	What this Companion has to offer
The study of psychology as a science	Throughout this Companion, we invite students to consider (and grapple with!) the scientific nature of psychology. We demonstrate how 'science' is ingrained with psychological, cultural, and contextual biases, and highlight work of feminist social psychologists who have made progress in challenging the rigid notion of science in psychology. This includes introducing related feminist concerns, such as reflexivity, bias, patriarchy, and intersectionality in research and theory
The social and cultural construction of psychology Conceptual and historical paradigms and models – comparisons and critiques	We take a social constructionist approach to social psychology throughout this Companion and encourage students to consider how theories that are thought to be 'objective' are actually reflective of certain dominant cultural and historical norms. We use this discussion to shine a light on efforts to decolonise social psychology throughout this Companion
Political and ethical issues in psychology	A concern for politics, ethics, and equality is echoed throughout this Companion

Table 3: Mapping this Companion to BPS core graduate skills

BPS core graduate skills	What this Companion has to offer
Apply multiple perspectives to psychological issues, recognising that psychology involves a range of research methods, theories, evidence, and applications	This Companion takes an explicitly creative and critical perspective towards social psychology and the mainstream curriculum. In this Companion, we fully acknowledge the legacy and merit of more traditional avenues of social psychological research, but also provide a critical stance. The Companion also covers more diverse, creative, and critical approaches to research. By introducing students to an alternative perspective on psychological issues, this Companion will broaden students' empirical and theoretical knowledge and skills

Table 3: (Continued)

BPS core graduate skills	What this Companion has to offer
Integrate ideas and findings across the multiple perspectives in psychology, and recognise distinctive psychological approaches to relevant issues	This Companion has been designed to introduce students to the multiple perspectives that exist within social psychology. We draw extensively upon ongoing issues and debates within social psychology, including discussions related to Open Science and the decolonisation of psychology
Generate and explore hypotheses and research questions drawing on relevant theory and research	Throughout this Companion, we provide interactive activities that serve to prompt students to generate their own ideas and questions about social psychology. In some instances, these activities are designed to be a starting point for the development of critical research questions, by encouraging students to take a critical, more open-minded view of the core mainstream approaches to the study of social psychology
Apply psychological knowledge ethically and safely to real-world problem	A concern for psychological literacy has been embedded into this Companion; for example, we often directly confront ethical, societal, and global problems, considering how students may use their new-found feminist knowledge to contribute meaningfully and responsibly to the 'greater good'. This is particularly pertinent in Chapter 9, where we aim to directly inspire activism and action, in light of the issues and debates that are highlighted throughout the Companion
Critically evaluate psychological theory and research	Reflective activities, discussion prompts, and 'See and hear for yourself' exercises have been included in this Companion to engage students in critical evaluation of the theories, approaches, and research methods within dominant areas of social psychology. To encourage students to think critically about these approaches, we provide alternative accounts and perspectives throughout, which draws upon a variety of research approaches

1 Introducing feminist social psychology

Welcome to our feminist world! In this the opening chapter, our aim is to give you a good start at using this book so you can make it your trusty companion. We will begin by 'setting out our pitch' – explaining what we hope this Companion book can achieve for you. If you have already followed a course on social psychology and feel you need to know more about how feminist theory and research fit in, then this will be right up your street. If, on the other hand, you are just starting out on your social psychology journey and want to incorporate a feminist perspective, then this book should hopefully give you a good grounding.

Let's begin by introducing ourselves. We are a bit of an odd combination but have found our co-authoring really enjoyable. We complement each other well because we each bring a slightly different angle to feminist social psychology. We met at a POWES conference – the British Psychological Society's (BPS) Psychology of Women and Equalities Section – and hit it off virtually during the COVID-19 lockdown. This book is the result of countless video-calls and excited email conversations over the course of the COVID pandemic. It certainly has been a labour of critical feminist love! We'll start this chapter by introducing you to the wonderful world of feminist social psychology, before spelling out the core reasons why we think this book will be beneficial to you on your social psychology journey.

Madeleine Pownall

Hello! I am a PhD researcher in social psychology, and I teach social psychology (among other things) in the School of Psychology at the University of Leeds. When Wendy first approached me about the prospect of co-writing a feminist 'retelling' of social psychology, I was thrilled. This is the book that I wish had been there for me when I was studying for my psychology degree at the University of Lincoln. I remember learning about critical social psychology with Dr Nathan Heflick and Dr Patrick Hylton and being fascinated by the glorious critical creativity of feminist social psychology. I was desperate to learn more, and so pored over Sue Wilkinson's *Feminist Social Psychologies* (1996) throughout my degree. Then, when I made the rather swift move from student to lecturer in 2018, I wanted my students to feel that excited 'burn' of feminist thinking in action that I had when reading Wilkinson's edited collection.

Wendy Stainton Rogers

Hello from me too. I'm what's known as a Professor Emerita, which is a posh way of saying I'm a retired woman professor who is still affiliated to the Open University where I worked for over forty years. My teaching was mainly in the Faculty of Health and Social Welfare, but most of my books are in Psychology, especially Critical Health and Social Psychology. Also, when I got into feminism in the 1980s, I taught Summer School on The OU's Women's Studies Course. So, unlike Madeleine, I discovered feminism after I completed my degree in 1964 and so I was really excited to be asked to write the first book in this series. What I bring to its authorship is a lot of experience, a pretty broad knowledge base, a background in pedagogy – the ology of teaching and learning – a real sense of fun, and the belief that academic study really doesn't have to be boring.

What is feminist social psychology?

> As feminists within psychology, we share major dissatisfaction with our discipline's fail-
> ure to engage with the lives of the majority of women, and the distortion and damage
> often produced when it does engage. We are committed to changing this and to devel-
> oping a psychology which properly represents women's concerns in all their diversity.
> However, more importantly, we are also committed to the deployment of such a psy-
> chology to address a range of social inequalities (including, for example, race and class,
> as well as gender) and to improve the conditions of women's lives: i.e., to feminism. We
> believe that in these twin purposes – the reconstruction of psychology and the impetus
> for social and political change – lies the radical potential of Feminism & Psychology.
> – Sue Wilkinson (1991, p. 5)

To first understand what we mean by *feminist psychology* generally, it is useful to consult the beating heart of feminist scholarship in psychology – the journal *Feminism & Psychology*. Our holy grail! We like how Sue Wilkinson describes the journal's aims above because it encompasses the two 'big projects' of feminist social psychology: (1) the fight against injustice, abuse, and inequality, and (2) the campaign to include women in the mainstream **discourses** of psychology. We will be unravelling the difference between these two lofty aims throughout this Companion, paying particular attention to the winding road of social psychology's history that has led to the emergence of feminist social psychology.

Feminist social psychology is ultimately concerned with the inclusion of women and girls into mainstream spaces, the advocacy of diverse and critical perspectives, and the fight for equality. However, it is important that we start this book with one clear clarification: feminist social psychology is absolutely not about 'men versus women'. (If only it was that simple!) Instead, feminist psychology is about identifying, exposing, theorising, and resolving inequalities and injustices. These may be injustices based on social class, race, ableism or, most commonly, gender. Feminist psychologists are all broadly committed to recognising the negative gendered consequences of the unequal distribution of power, ***patriarchy***, the ***sexist*** nature of social norms, and ***intersectionality***. While feminist thought can be embedded throughout psychology, social psychology is 'where many feminist psychologists find a natural home' (Thompson, 2017, p. 2). Because of this, Bernice Lott argues that 'a feminist perspective is not only compatible with the history, objectives, and emphases of social psychology, but necessary for its continued vitality' (1991, p. 505).

To start to get us thinking about what we are trying to *achieve* in this Companion, let's look at (what we consider to be) the five cornerstones of feminist social psychology:

1. Gender is actively and socially constructed

While feminist social psychology investigates all kinds of facets of human experience and is not limited to the study of gender *itself*, feminist social psychologists have advocated strongly over the years for the need to explore how gender gets *socially constructed* by society. Throughout this Companion, we will continually think back to the many 'gender/sex' discussions that feminist social psychologists have become embroiled in over the years. As Janis S. Bohan points out, there are generally two approaches to the study and understanding of gender which feminist psychology should consider. The first is an essentialist approach to gender, which views gender in terms of a fundamental, internal quality that is fixed and unmoving. As Bohan puts it, essentialists view gender as being 'resident within the individual' (1993, p. 6), seen as entirely separate from a person's ongoing experiences, social context, or any external pressures or influences. Social constructionists, by contrast, argue that gender is not a fixed internal entity, but is in fact a 'societally made' aspect of one's person, which is related to the societal gendering of particular 'transactions' and 'performances' that are understood to be sex-specific. We much prefer the latter of these two approaches, which you will come to learn as you journey with us through this Companion.

A social constructionist approach to gender involves challenging the assumption that gender operates as a binary (i.e. man vs. woman) and instead celebrates the more fluid construction of gender operating in a particular society, at a particular time, in a particular situation. This shift away from a binary view of gender also offers feminist social psychologists the capacity to examine diverse femininities, masculinities, and the myriad *performances* of gender, which we'll look at in a lot more detail in Chapters 7 and 8. This conversation about the social construction of gender has been happening for a while now, since, for example, the sociologists West and Zimmerman (1987) wrote about the act of 'doing gender' and highlighted that gender is enacted continuously in everyday social interactions.

Importantly, by acknowledging that gender is a product created through social construction, and by dismantling the idea of a distinct binary of men/women, this allows feminist psychology to recognise and celebrate the experiences of people whose gender identity is not reconcilable with a binary understanding of sex. Therefore, given that feminist social psychology aims to include, acknowledge, listen to, and make life better for *all* people, feminist psychologists recognise diverse gender identities. There is a strong ongoing debate about the rise of **TERFs** (trans-exclusionary radical feminists), which we will come to later in this Companion too.

2. Women's lives are rich, nuanced sources of information that should not be overlooked in mainstream psychological scholarship

Feminist social psychology is primarily concerned with ensuring that women's lived experiences, in all their messy, complicated glory, are not marginalised from mainstream social psychology. Historically, as we will point out throughout this Companion, research is – and certainly *was* – often centred almost exclusively around the male experience (Carlson & Carlson, 1960), and the early research on women's experiences was typically discussed with **androcentric** (or male-centric) language. As Fine and Gordon explain, 'traditionally, women have been the *objects* of these conversations [in psychology], but not their *subjects*', which has led feminist psychologists to start a process of 'reclaiming the topic of girls and women' (1991, p. 19). To reflect this concern, in this Companion, we will offer you a 'reclaimed' version of psychology's history, examining phenomena such as the way male voices dominate mainstream psychology (Crawford & Marecek, 1989), the problematic nature of androcentrism or male-centrism (Bailey, LaFrance, & Dovidio, 2020), and the value of the contribution made by women and minoritised groups to the study of psychology (Thompson, 2017).

Feminist researchers have also highlighted in this 'missing history' a concern over what is *not* being recorded, which may in some instances be even more important (and problematic) than that which *is* being recorded. For example, scholars have noted how there is a historical and persisting lack of data on maternal deaths among minority women in the USA (D'Ignazio & Klein, 2020). This has only recently been given national attention thanks to concerted efforts by Black-women-led reproductive justice groups (e.g. SisterSong). We will come onto this issue of missing voices in Chapter 2 and Chapter 4, and will share some wider examples of activist groups who aim to reclaim these voices in Chapter 9.

3. Research is inherently political and subjective

Throughout their long legacy, feminist social psychologists have prompted social psychology to critically consider the questions that we ask (Rutherford, 2007), and to start a process of learning to 'inquire about how we inquire' (Ackerly & True, 2008, p. 695). By this, they mean that feminist research should avoid taking anything for granted and relying on established norms of 'how we do things'. For example, whenever a social psychologist designs a study, collects data from participants, runs analyses, and reports the results, none of this constitutes an objective process. There will always be a *reason* that this particular research question is considered interesting in the first place. There will always be a decision made about the nature of the participants chosen, the form of data collection used, the kinds of analysis adopted. These are not objective, detached, apolitical processes. After all, they can't be, because these decisions are actively and purposely made by human beings!

As we will uncover throughout the Companion, the wryly cautious stance that we feminists take about claims of 'objectivity' ultimately leads us to recognise the importance of *reflexivity* as a feminist tool. As Lazard and McAvoy explain in their wonderfully practical paper, reflexivity is based around asking oneself the question, 'what is the research process and how am I influencing it?' (2020, p. 167). This questioning forms part of an ongoing process that prompts the researcher to continually shift and (re)construct their understanding, as part of a process that Wilkinson (1988) calls 'disciplined self-reflection'. For example, in her APA presidential address of 1989, Ellen B. Kimmel reported the findings from an open-ended questionnaire survey which asked feminist psychologists about their experiences of feminism. From a subsequent discussion, Kimmel reflected on the process: 'I am convinced through my own experience, and that of others who have described theirs, that the personal is not only political or professional, but also scientific. That a valid source of truth about human beings and their existence is themselves as they tell it' (1989, p. 144). Feminist social psychologists have made some great progress in acknowledging how the values of traditional 'science' may not be wholly compatible with a feminist approach to studying human beings.

Similarly, Alice Eagly and Stephanie Riger also provide a thorough appraisal of feminist methodologies and *epistemologies* in psychology, and they note how researchers' 'values and social contexts, their selectivity in evaluating evidence, and the flaws of their methods receive little consideration' (2014, p. 686). The authors critique the notion that psychological research is fully 'objective' (i.e. detached, scientific, not affected by personal views), and instead advocate for an appreciation of how norms and biases guide the research process. This has been an important part of feminist social psychology's agenda.

4. Feminism needs to be intersectional

> Building global feminisms and transnational linkages is a complex process when there is no one 'local', 'national', or 'global' woman, nor any single universal 'feminist' approach. (Flew et al., 1999, p. 402)

As we will explore throughout this Companion, *intersectionality* is a cornerstone of feminist social psychological thinking and research. This will be particularly present in Chapters 3 and 5. This theory, or theoretical framework, has its roots in Black feminist activism and scholarship, demonstrating how our investigations of inequality should acknowledge the 'interlocking systems of oppression' that different groups of people face (Rosenthal, 2016). Examining *intersectionality* shows, for example, how the sexism and oppression that Black women face is markedly different from the form of sexism that White women face. In light of this, intersectionality scholars such as Lillian Comas-Díaz have noted the 'dynamic interplay' between feminism and ethnicism (i.e. the movement to promote equality among people of difference ethnic and racial groups). As Comas-Díaz puts it, ethnicism 'stresses the pervasive interaction of ethnicity, culture, race, gender, discrimination, and oppression in the lives of people of color' (1991, p. 598).

Social psychology has long been criticised for being ethnocentric, of constructing theories and doing research based on the assumption that 'we' – that is, people like 'us' – reflect the only society and/or culture around. Psychology is purported to be the study of global humankind, but has, until very recently, actually been little more than a form of anthropology – one in which just one society/culture takes centre-stage! Feminist social psychologists have stressed that our feminist thinking needs to look far beyond our own specific national, regional, and cultural contexts (see Eagly et al., 2012). In response to these concerns, social psychologists have proposed phrases such as the ***majority world*** and the ***minority world***. Promoted by Shahidul Alam, this division avoids judgemental terms like 'Developing world' and 'Third World' – obscuring the economic and social impact of colonialism and economic exploitation on parts of the world (the majority) that are as a consequence lacking in resources and power.

5. Feminist social psychologists should work to decolonise psychology

It is important throughout feminist social psychology discussion that we look beyond the experiences and viewpoints of women in the Global North, as these experiences are 'insufficiently attentive to the dynamics of coloniality and uneven flows of global power' (Rutherford, 2021, p. 35). Calls to '***decolonise***' social psychology go back to the late 1980s, when feminist scholars began to actively critique theories of gender that were only conceptualised 'for' and 'with' Western women (Rutherford, 2021). More recently, Linda Tuhiwai Smith (2013) has advocated for decolonial methodologies in feminist psychology, and Glen Jankowski (2020) has been an influential voice in working to decolonise the teaching of psychology.

A good example of where we need to go is a recent paper by Tuğçe Kurtiş and Glenn Adams (2015) that looks specifically about the need for feminist psychology to be decolonised. They observe that while feminist and postcolonial standpoints both share a common commitment to liberation, feminist psychology is 'not always compatible with, and at times even contradictory to global struggles for decolonization'. As they scathingly point out, feminist scholarship must not be restricted to 'freeing some women to better participate in global domination' (2015, p. 388).

Feminist trouble-making

As you can imagine, critical feminist approaches are more in-your-face and controversial than the mainstream. Being critical here is not about being carping and negative, though it can feel like that sometimes. It is more of a deliberately cynical act that contests the veracity and fairness of the status quo. To be critical in this context is to throw down the gauntlet to the comfy, smug version of the-world-according-to-patriarchy. We will explain the intricacies of patriarchy explicitly in Chapter 3. A paper by Carol Tavris provides an excellent illustration of making this kind of trouble. She begins like this, exhorting us to:

> ... transcend the literal and limited question of 'Do men and women differ?' and ask instead: Why is everyone so interested in differences? Which differences? And what function does the belief in differences serve? ... to consider where our theories come from, who benefits from them and where they lead us. (Tavris, 1993, p. 151)

You can see the edge that criticality has added to the way she asks awkward questions, ones that challenge the foundations of social psychology's research and theory-building, in a decidedly sceptical and suspicious way. Crucially, she asks questions about power – who has it, for what purposes are they using it, and to what ends? She introduces the term 'bias' into the equation and accuses male psychologists of distorting what is going on through the terminology they use.

Tavris (1993) draws on research by Carol Olson (1988) on the *female modesty effect*' to make her point (see also Heatherington et al., 1993). Olson bases this effect on psychological research purporting to show that:

• women have lower self-esteem than men do;
• women do not value their own efforts as much as men do;
• women are less self-confident than men.

What Tavris does in her paper is to re-write this list by reversing the claims – for example, instead of women's lower self-esteem, what we should conclude is that 'men are more conceited than women'. She relocates the problem within male behaviour rather than that of women.

Tavris goes on to say how liberating she found it to re-word the throw-away lines she heard in everyday life that treated women as lacking, problematic, or just plain weird – what we have come to call *gaslighting* – and locating the lack/problem/weirdness in men instead:

> Women are not 'gullible'; men are inflexible. Women are not 'humorless'; men do not know what is funny. Women are not 'emotionally immature' for remaining attached to their parents throughout life; men are 'emotionally inhibited' from expressing their continuing needs for their family. (Tavris, 1993, p. 152)

This reversal-of-the-problem is a deliciously neat ruse you can use to challenge the things men (and sometimes women) say that act as a massive put-down to women. Call them out by offering this kind of counter. When we do, we see it as our own personal crusade against women's self-esteem being constantly under attack. Give it a try, see it as the start of your journey to becoming a *feminist killjoy*' – to use Sara Ahmed's (2010) popular term – whatever your gender.

Our feminist manifesto – what feminism can do

Now that we know about the fundamental agenda and purpose of feminist social psychology, let's explore the core reasons why we think this Companion book will be useful to you. Feminist approaches to social psychology are becoming increasingly popular, but we do still exist firmly on the 'margins' of the discipline. Feminist social psychologists have made real progress over the years, but there is still much work to be done! Ultimately, we hope that this Companion will introduce you to new ways of thinking, uncover some new perspectives on the core social psychology curriculum you are following/ have followed, and (importantly) lead you into having some critical feminist fun!

Reason 1: A feminist Companion can debunk the myths about and misunderstandings of feminism

Blythe Baird, a **slam poet** and feminist, once said: 'there are times I want people to like me more than I want to change the world'. We should note early on that there are some pervasive stereotypes about being a 'feminist killjoy' that can feel onerous and disheartening. Feminism is very often misunderstood because of the promotion of 'fake facts' – that feminists are all ugly, hairy, and aggressively anti-men. They are pitiful women who moan all the time, complaining about stuff that is fine as it is. It's certainly true that we feminists get angry at the state of the world, especially in relation to all the gender-based violence, inequalities, and injustices that exist. And not surprisingly, we are frustrated by all the unfairness out there – such as systematically being paid less and being expected to take on the bulk of childcare when the going gets tough. Yet, in reality, feminism is much more a matter of wanting to make everyone's life-worlds better – fairer, kinder, better organised; more compassionate, generous, and accepting of diversity. We hope that this Companion will help to debunk some of the myths surrounding feminism itself and will crucially demonstrate how feminism is not a nasty plot, but simply a different lens through which to view the world.

Reason 2: A feminist Companion can open up new ways of seeing (and hearing)

Adopting a feminist perspective on social psychology can help you to radically open up your perception to enable you to explore new ideas, to adopt new perspectives, to consider new possibilities, and to pursue new and exciting horizons. You will be led away from seeing things through a **'male gaze'** (a distinctly masculine way of seeing or doing) and introduced to a new feminist lens through which hidden things, such as injustice and exploitation, become more visible. This is a process of becoming dis-*illusioned*, a recognition that not everything is as it is claimed to be – that, for example, women are not *naturally* destined to be mothers, or have brains that inevitably go bonkers during pregnancy.

Reason 3: A feminist Companion can help us do what needs to be done to make the world a better place

Overwhelmingly, feminism is a *practical* endeavour. Whilst feminist scholars have and do made serious progress in developing highly sophisticated theory, their purpose goes well beyond gaining intellectual satisfaction. It is highly pragmatic, with a keen sense of what is worth investing in for the greater good, and when to fight certain battles another day. It is always directed towards social activism, even if not always directly. In Chapter 9, once we have walked you through the various theoretical standpoints and research on feminist social psychology, we will end by examining some good examples of feminist social psychology 'in action'. This can crucially differentiate feminist social psychology from more mainstream approaches, because we always have our sights firmly set on activism and 'real-world' change.

Reason 4: A feminist Companion can show you how to act responsibly and ethically

Feminism can help to make you become more 'psychologically literate', which is an important outcome for any psychology education. Psychological literacy is a 'new wave' in psychology education that has come to light in the past few years; as Cranney and colleagues (2011) explain, psychological literacy is about students' ability to adaptively and intentionally apply psychology to meet personal, professional, and societal needs. It is about taking the 'stuff" you learn about psychology beyond the lecture theatre and using it meaningfully and responsibly to contribute to solving important global problems and 'big issues', such as gender equality, sustainability, and human rights. Feminist theory and research has become acutely conscious of the need for social psychologists to be responsible, ethical citizens at a global level. The Companion will help you gain the knowledge and skills required to actively pursue *social justice* outcomes, in ways that treat everyone with respect, promote accessibility, and counter exclusion. It is historically aware and sensitive to the long-term impact of colonisation. It encourages humility and seeks to resolve the harms engendered by hierarchy.

Reason 5: A feminist Companion can help you to find the fun in being a feminist

Despite the ambitions to 'do good and be ethical', being a feminist social psychologist in no way condemns you to living, feeling, or acting miserably. Sara Ahmed (2010; Ahmed & Bonis, 2012) argues that we must have the courage to call out misbehaviour – even when this involves becoming 'a feminist killjoy'. But she also recognises that feminism works by women (and their male allies) supporting and encouraging each other, sharing moments of joy arising from 'righting wrongs', and simply having the staying power to keep showing that there are other (kinder and more respectful) ways to do leadership, work collectively, support our communities, judge value – and even tackle pandemics!

Also note that when feminists get together for mutual support, there is generally a lot of laughter and fun. If you want to see it in action, do come to a POWES conference if you can (there are bursaries).

CHAPTER SUMMARY

- In this chapter, we have introduced you to the goals of feminist social psychology, identifying how a feminist approach to social psychology centres broadly around a concern for inequality and social justice.
- Feminist social psychology advocates for a view of psychology that acknowledges intersectionality, social constructionism, patriarchy, and power.
- We have identified five core reasons why we think this Companion will be useful to you. Now that we have a shared understanding of what feminist social psychology is trying to do, we can start to interrogate, unravel, and rethink teachings from mainstream social psychology.

2 How (and why) is social psychology changing?

Learning objectives

Study of this chapter (including its activities) should enable you to:

- Start to unravel some of social psychology's history, gaining insights into how feminist social psychology has been constructed.
- Begin to gain an understanding about the shifts that have occurred within social psychology from it being seen as a scientific endeavour to viewing it as a more interpretative one – where the aim is not to discover facts but to gain insight and understanding.
- Know more about the different approaches that feminist social psychologists take in their research, ranging from experimental methods to more participatory, 'newer' ways of doing research.
- Understand the term 'reflexivity' and how it relates to feminist social psychological research.
- Recognise the dramatic changes in social psychology evidenced by the contributions of both Muzafer and Carolyn Sherif. This should include knowledge of the theoretical, methodological, and ethical problems to social psychology's early field experiments.
- Begin thinking critically and creatively about the possibilities of social psychology through a feminist lens.

The early days of social psychology

In order to understand where social psychology is *going* (and how we can help it get there!), we first need to uncover some of the field's murky history – though this is mainly covered in Chapter 4. Social psychology has always been concerned with prejudice, conflict, and attitudes, ever since Kurt Lewin started studying leadership and personality in the 1930s. After this early work, social psychologists continued to be fascinated with how groups are formed, how they interact, how identity is constructed, and how people go about trying to live together in peace. In the 1970s and 1980s, feminist psychologists began sowing the seeds for a major paradigm shift within social psychology. Since then, our discipline has also undergone shifts in the way it approaches the study of the human condition. This chapter will explore some of these shifts, providing you with a different way of viewing social psychology's history (and reclaiming an equally influential **her-story**).

Although the terminology, methods, and philosophy underpinning the discipline are continually shifting – we'll look into this throughout this chapter – there are some areas of research that have remained at the forefront of the social psychology agenda. Intergroup conflict is a good example. In 1954, Muzafer Sherif conducted one of the most famous and widely-cited field experiments in social psychology.

The story goes that over three weeks in the Robbers Cave State Park in Oklahoma, USA, twenty-two boys attended a 'summer camp' that was, in fact, a social psychology experiment. The boys were split into two groups: the 'Rattlers' and the 'Eagles'. At the beginning of the study, the two groups were kept apart, with each group of boys spending time bonding together in what Sherif referred to as the 'ingroup formation' stage. Once suitably 'formed', Sherif had the two groups of boys compete against each other in a series of games, the winners of which received a prize. This was dubbed the 'friction' phase, as it aimed to develop intergroup competition. A fair amount of hostility and aggression was evident between the two groups, which Sherif considered to be 'realistic group conflict' – or, as he called it, 'intergroup conflict'. This was a demonstration of what happens when social groups compete for resources. In simple terms, groups demonstrate conflict when they compete for tangible, real resources. Importantly, however, Sherif theorised that this conflict can be overcome if the groups are brought together to achieve a common goal.

Groups and intergroup conflict

'Groups' are messy, complicated things. A group may be a selection of random people brought together to do a study, or it may be based on broad and diverse demographics (such as being a group of football fans). Some of the earliest experiments in social psychology showed how easy it is to create group membership, no matter how flimsy the grouping is! Importantly, membership of a group does not require strong allegiance to one's social identity. For example, if you are randomly assigned to be in Group A of an experiment, it is unlikely that membership of that group will be tied closely to your overall *sense of self*. However, much of our own self-concept, or sense of self, is strongly tied to group membership – such as being a member of a group of feminist psychologists.

Social psychologists are interested in the formation, development, and sustainment of group cohesion because of the insights provided into what happens when groups interact, particularly in the context of *conflict*. It is worth noting here that the original Robber Cave experiment was an entirely male affair – only boys took part, and all the experimenters were also male. Donna Haraway pointed out that when she started as a lowly assistant in primatology, it was much the same. The men were in charge, and their accounts of apes' and monkeys' social lives were all about dominance hierarchies and defending territory. It wasn't until women began to design research in the field that the focus shifted to nurture and cooperation among the females (Haraway, 1986).

Viv Burr and Margie Wetherell provide good illustrations of a feminist social psychological approach to the study of groups and identities. Burr is best known for her very accessible books on social constructionism (e.g. 2015), whilst Wetherell is the co-author (with Jonathan Potter) of *Discourse and Social Psychology: Beyond Attitudes and Behaviour* (1987), which introduces social psychology to the concept of **discourse** and the analytics of discourse analysis.

Missing *her*-stories?

The Robbers Cave experiment, like many other social psychology studies of the 1950s and 1960s, is considered a classic. It remains a staple of the A-level Psychology curriculum and of mainstream core teaching because it provides such a neat illustration of how conflict can arise. Despite the significance and legacy of this early work, however, as with much of the history of social psychology, textbooks do not always capture the full story.

A less well-known contributor to the famous Robbers Cave experiment was Muzafer Sherif's long-standing collaborator and colleague, Carolyn Wood Sherif – who (you guessed it!) just happened to be his wife. Perhaps unsurprisingly, especially if you consider that, despite her efforts, Carolyn was unable to attend Princeton University because she was a woman, it is the contribution of her 'pioneer' husband to these classic studies that is best known. In the early days of the Sherifs' 'intergroup conflict' theory, Carolyn was struggling to build a career for herself, although much of her husband's work was done in collaboration with her. This was because she was busy bringing up their three daughters, who were born a few years before the study began.

Carolyn's battle introduces us to the notion of the **motherhood penalty**, which is a consequence of **patriarchy**. Women's careers were (and still are) halted by motherhood, despite their ability to prove their competence and commitment (Benard & Correll, 2010). It remains an insidious and near universal reality for women, based on evidence from studies conducted in dozens of countries. The penalty arises from the perception that a 'woman's place' is in the home, an idea perpetuated by gender stereotypes that are both *descriptive* (they describe how different people occupy different social roles) and *prescriptive* (they dictate how people *should* act, in light of these roles).

Most notably in the Sherifs' story is how, once their children had grown up, Carolyn successfully made a name for herself as a feminist social psychologist. She advocated strongly for critical approaches to psychology and prompted social psychologists to rethink the contextless 'objectivity' within which social research had been situated. And in 1998 she was to write one of the first papers on bias in social psychology – a very powerful polemic indeed! Years later, feminist psychologists continue to complain about how psychology is biased (e.g. Eagly & Riger, 2014)

See and hear for yourself

If you have the time, a great way to get your head round the complex history of this experiment is to read Gina Perry's book: *The Lost Boys: Inside Muzafer Sherif's Robbers Cave Experiment* (2019). Note that it is a commercial biography and just one person's account of what happened. But it's a fascinating story about what psychology was like in the 1950s and 1960s.

ACTIVITY 2.1: Carolyn Wood Sherif's feminist psychology timeline

Carolyn Wood Sherif had a fascinating career that spoke to all kinds of inequalities within social psychology and society more generally. Documenting this 'lost' history of feminist scholars is an important part of a feminist agenda. In 2010, a group of feminist psychologists led by Professor Alexandra Rutherford, a feminist psychologist and Professor of Historical, Theoretical, and Critical Study of Psychology, launched the 'Psychology's Feminist Voices' project. The project aims to document the contributions that women have made to psychology, using archive materials and oral history interviews.

1 Visit the Psychology's Feminist Voices project website (www.feministvoices. com). Take some time browsing the website, as it's a wonderful resource that is teeming with juicy history from psychology's early days.
2 Locate the biography page of Carolyn Wood Sherif.
3 On a large piece of paper map out a timeline of Carolyn's life and work. You might find it helpful to flag the pivotal points in her career in different colours.

Some things to consider:

- What do you notice about Carolyn's career progression?
- What were key moments on her journey to becoming a 'feminist killjoy'? This is a term Sara Ahmed (2010) coined for women who are prepared to speak out and to 'rock the boat' in the interests of a feminist agenda – we'll explore this term properly in Chapter 9.
- Looking at your university or organisation, what challenges remain for women, and do Carolyn's actions offer some solutions?

SECTION SUMMARY

- We have discussed some of the core findings from social psychology and have started the process of reappraising the discipline's history, paying particular attention to who is missing from it.
- Feminist psychology has begun re-examining social psychology's murky history to highlight the contributions of feminist psychologists that were previously side-lined due to 'the motherhood penalty' and patriarchal norms.
- It is an important duty of contemporary feminist psychologists to 'reclaim' the *her*-story of psychology's past: as per the Psychology's Feminist Voice project.

See and hear for yourself

You can repeat the above activity for any of the profiles on the Psychology's Feminist Voices project website. Throughout the remainder of this book, whenever we mention a particularly influential feminist psychologist, look them up on the PFV website and do a bit more digging into their history. You'll be amazed at the detail of some of the accounts – true feminist activism in action!

Social cognition

Social cognition, which has always been a major topic in social psychology, can be summarised as follows:

Attention: How people strategically direct their attention to what matters, and respond to signs of danger.

Perception: The way we perceive what we see, hear, smell, and feel in the world around us, including other people and ourselves, and how we make sense of it all.

Memory: How we store our perceptions, thoughts, and ideas in our memory – and how we remember them when we need to.

Reasoning and problem-solving: How we work out problems – such as finding something that you've lost, making plans, achieving goals, and playing games.

You will likely have studied cognition as a topic in its own right already. But to understand its place in feminist social psychology, there are some key points you need to understand.

Attention: As thoughtful cognitive beings, we are highly active in the way they think. We don't just take in sensory information in the way a camera automatically replicates the light patterns that it captures. Human thinking is highly strategic, and is therefore highly selective in what it bothers to capture.

Perception: Similarly, human perception is processed not by reference to what is actually in front of you but by what has been 'burned into' your memory. You do not see a camera copy, but rather you recognise whatever it is from what is already powerfully familiar to you. In other words, you 'think fast' (Kahneman, 2011) by mainly relying on what you already know.

Memory: But the downside of processing being so efficient is that thinking like this is unreliable, and you make lots of mistakes. Your memories act like templates, often called schemas or stereotypes, that allow you to recognise what you are dealing with.

Reasoning and problem-solving: By contrast, we have the capacity to reason in an active, careful, and meticulous manner, and by making thinking conscious and purposeful, we can 'think slow' (Kahneman, 2011). This is what we mean by giving you a 'feminist lens' – a way of looking at the world in an actively questioning way; one that is wary about having the 'wool pulled over our eyes' and being prepared to do detective work to find out what is *really* going on.

Why cognitive compromise matters

A good example from mainstream social psychology – the fundamental attribution error – is the recognition that the people that psychologists study (i.e. in the minority world) have a tendency to blame other people when things go wrong, rather than recognise that it may be more a matter of circumstances. However, in feminist social psychology, it is **unconscious bias** that matters most, an inherent element in all human thinking. Bias creeps into processes that people believe to be objective and stable and it is not until we get them to confront these assumptions and biases that we can begin to unravel the cord that ties it all so neatly together. People view the world through a lens that is moulded by where they live, what they experience, and who they are. This means that, as a by-product of being a living, breathing human, we all of us are biased about everything, all the time. Therefore, as Alice Eagly (2012) suggests, the implicit biases of social psychologists make the study of humans very difficult, particularly in the context of investigating gendered phenomena – very dodgy indeed! It's a bit like trying to push a bus up a hill while you are simultaneously a passenger in it. Implicit biases are slippery things; they are deeply embedded attitudes, assumptions, and stereotypes that cloud our judgement without us being consciously aware or our error. Eagly warns that implicit biases lead us to interpret human behaviour in a way that makes it 'fit' with our previously held views about gender, which can be fuelled by structural issues such as patriarchy.

Being led astray

If we are to become responsible consumers of social psychology, and to actively exercise our feminist thinking, we need to recognise what is going on and how to confront it. For example, in social psychology, it is important to be mindful of the effects of *naive realism*. This refers to the fallacy whereby we believe our own experience of reality is the *only* true version, as it feels so very 'right' to us. We see other versions as nonsensical, faulty, harmful, or just plain wrong. Social psychologists are not exempt from these kinds of judgement errors, biases, or misperceptions. Progress within psychology will be brought to a halt if psychological researchers believe that their own version of reality, as informed by their own lived experience, is the only 'acceptable' or 'correct' narrative.

This is similar to the idea of confirmation bias, a social psychology classic, which shows how people actively seek out information that confirms what they believe to be true (Nickerson, 1998). Social psychology teaches us that our 'self-concept' (the way we see ourselves) may be heavily influenced by external ideas. Due to this fragility of self-concept, we constantly strive to *confirm* – as opposed to *challenge* – our '*worldview*'. Goodwin (2010) provides a useful example of how easily we can kid ourselves that the world is organised in a way that is in accordance with our personal beliefs. If a person firmly believes that they have a sixth sense, or that they are able to intuitively predict events before they occur, this belief is reaffirmed (or *confirmed*) whenever something happens that feels spookily coincidental, even if it is just a coincidence. It is theorised as an adaptive mechanism which allows us to feel that the social world is organised in a way that is predictable, and neither threatening nor uncomfortable.

Naive realism and confirmation bias demonstrate how the 'truth' in science is entrenched with psychological, cultural, and contextual biases. However, most social psychologists like to think of themselves as detached observers of phenomena. If you Google 'scientist', you will invariably be met with stock images of white men wearing lab coats and carrying test tubes. Given the prevalence of this image, psychologists who do not 'fit' this stereotype tend not to be taken seriously. This is because the notion of a 'scientist' has been constructed by something or someone to fit a certain set of values and attributes. It has been socially constructed to mean something specific.

ACTIVITY 2.2: Design a bias-free psychology experiment

Imagine that you are a social psychologist interested in *replicating* the Robbers Cave experiment – we'll talk more about replication in social psychology in Chapter 6. Your aim is to conduct the same study as the Sherifs in a modern context with you as the principal social psychology researcher. Map out your study design on a piece of paper. Think about the various variables, the things you might need to control for, the outcomes.

Now, once you have removed all risk of bias from your proposed design, work through the following prompt questions to yourself.

Prompt questions:

1 Who are *you* as the researcher? What kinds of assumptions do you carry about the world that could infect the data with bias?
2 What do you expect to find? Do you think these expectations have informed the study design?
3 How were your measures chosen? Where did you find them? Do all researchers have access to these, or do you have insider knowledge?

4 How can you recruit participants in a way that is as open, fair, and accessible as possible? Do some groups of people get excluded? Why?

5 Say you run your study, collect data, and find results that confirm your hypothesis. What does this mean for the study of the human condition?

6 Who benefits from this research? Who does it have capacity to harm?

For example, your responses may prompt you to consider how your own gender/race/background has led you to think that these questions are 'interesting'. As Magnusson and Marecek note, 'knowledge is "interested": that is, there is a reason why a particular question is of interest' (2012, p. 90). What they mean by this is that research questions are never neutral or 'apolitical'. They were *considered* interesting by a researcher for a specific reason. In this activity, we want you to start to really interrogate the reasons why we deem something 'interesting'. This will (hopefully) allow us to move away from the *voyeuristic* way of doing research: where you pick a participant group that you have no affiliation with, 'intrude their space', collect data, and hop it, never to be seen again. The more you consider how your background, your biases, and your assumptions guide the research process, the better a feminist social psychologist you will be!

A feminist approach to bias

You may have finished the above activity thinking that psychology is doomed because of the pervasive bias that seeps in at every single turn of the research process. As a social psychologist, you are now left with two options:

Option 1: you work to remove as much as this pesky bias as possible. You design experiments that are robust, replicable, and valid. You conduct studies in padded cells with no other social 'noise' possible. You call yourself an objective, 'proper' scientist, much like a physicist – indeed, in some quarters the strive to be scientific is called '*physics envy*'!

Option 2: you recognise that bias is an omnipresent part of research, so you opt to centre and celebrate the existence of such bias in your research. You write your papers openly and transparently, noting how your experiences, demographics, and assumptions are likely to creep into the research process. And your results will need to be interpreted with this in mind. You reflect upon how bias shapes our research.

By incorporating the latter option into research, we are acknowledging (and celebrating!) bias. As influential feminist psychologists such as Alice Eagly and Carolyn Sherif have argued, bias is not the enemy. Rather, bias is the 'thing' that unites human experience. Jeanne Marecek (2019) offers a synthesis of Sherif's approach to bias, which demonstrates beautifully how the study of social psychology should be approached differently from other 'hard science' subjects.

Sherif offered a lengthy criticism of the idea that 'controlled' experiments can succeed in extracting participants (and experimenters) from their historical, social, cultural, and interpersonal contexts. A human individual, she argued, cannot be studied by the same methods as a 'chemical compound' ... like many other feminist social scientists, she argued that such context-stripping was based on highly restricted notions of science. (Marecek, 2019, p. 425)

This introduces us to the idea of **_reflexivity_** – which, ultimately, is the process of engaging deeply in a form of self-reflection about who we are as researchers, how our biases guide and inform the research process, and how our worldview is shaped by the research we do (Wilkinson, 1988). Reflexivity is an important part of a feminist social psychologist's toolkit and is inherently concerned with an appreciation of subjectivity (as opposed to objectivity), bias, and positionality. Feminist psychologists have proposed innovative new methods for the study of social psychology. This approach to research considers the role of reflexivity, which is the process of deep self-reflection on how who we are as people informs the research we do. There are broadly two 'types' of reflexivity:

Personal reflexivity involves a consideration of how aspects of the researcher's own identity, such as personal values, background, experiences, and interests, shapes the research itself. In other words, personal reflexivity demonstrates how who we are as people informs what we choose to spend our time studying as psychologists. As Jill Lepore summarises beautifully (2011): 'No social science is more extravagantly autobiographical than psychology'. By this, she means that what we choose to study, and indeed how we choose to study it, is informed by our own journey _to_ and _through_ psychology.

Functional reflexivity shifts the focus away from the researcher and onto the research itself and is concerned with reflection on the form that social psychology takes. Functional reflexivity here involves a continuously critical examination of the practices and processes of research, with the aim of revealing its assumptions, values, and biases.

SECTION SUMMARY

- Feminist psychologists have proposed innovative new methods for the study of social psychology. This approach to research considers the role of reflexivity, which is the process of deep self-reflection on how who we are as a person informs the research that we do as social psychologists.
- Feminist research celebrates bias in a way that mainstream approaches are not used to doing. Instead of shying away from bias and attempting to ignore it, feminist methodologies typically centre and celebrate it.
- We have introduced you to the important concept of reflexivity, which is a hallmark of feminist social psychological methodology. Given that reflexivity prompts us to question who we are as a researcher and how we're informing the research process, this dismantles some of the assumptions of mainstream, quantitative, laboratory-based social psychology that operates under a veneer of objectivity.

What (and who) is social psychology for?

In August of 2020, in the immediate aftermath of the worldwide Black Lives Matter protests, *The Psychologist* magazine published a letter in which a psychologist complained about an anti-racist statement by the British Psychological Society (Miller, 2020). The letter took issue with the society's value statement on racism, noting that an anti-racism statement serves to (problematically) tell psychologists 'what we should believe'. *Social justice*, apparently, is beyond the remit of psychological 'science'. Predictably, this sparked a discipline-wide flurry of online responses, furiously debating whether psychology should concern itself with 'social justice' discussions. The responses came broadly from two perspectives, the first insisting that psychology as a profession should be a detached, objective version of science that does not succumb to the messy, often subjective nature of social justice agendas. The second, much more frequently expressed, perspective was one that celebrates psychology's capacity for social good. This conversation raises some important questions about what (and who) psychology should be *for*. Some psychologists have expressed concerns that we are 'giving psychology away' to the masses, and that the credibility of the discipline is under threat (Lewis & Wai, 2020).

In recent years, largely fuelled by the rise of qualitative methodologies that centre *lived experience* in psychology, the relationship between social justice, equality, politics, and social psychology has been revisited. Since the Sherifs first set about understanding how conflict arises in social situations, social psychology has been tangled up with the messiness of social justice. Therefore, the idea that social psychology should (or even can) be detached and removed from the 'subjective' (which is, after all, the enemy of objective science!) is a difficult sell. As we will discuss throughout this book, our *lived experiences* are informed by the various 'intersecting' social identities that we occupy. We will cover the idea of intersectionality in a lot more detail in Chapter 3.

A NOTE ON INTERSECTIONALITY

Intersectionality is a term that derives from Black feminist ideas and describes how our social identities exist within 'interlocking systems of oppression' and structures of (in)equalities (Crenshaw, 1991). It highlights how intersecting oppressed identities carry with them certain social expectations and norms. Importantly, intersectionality is rooted in a concern for social justice, stigma, and structural oppression, all of which are cornerstones of feminist social psychology. We'll discuss this in much more depth in Chapter 3.

Moving forward

In 1984, Audre Lorde, a Black feminist, activist, and poet, famously authored an essay that exposed the social world as occupying a space she called 'the master's house' – a patriarchal, misogynistic, male paradise, one that serves to silence and trivialise women's experiences. As well as being a beautifully crafted piece of literature that demonstrates the power of patriarchy and inequalities, the essay also pointed to the capacity for social change through a lens of both feminism and anti-racism. Lorde's core idea is that trying to dismantle a system while being *within it* is tricky (a bit like trying to push that bus up a hill, while being a passenger on it), if not impossible. We cannot attempt to rethink and restructure an establishment by living and being inside of it. She writes:

> ... the master's tools will never dismantle the master's house. They may allow us temporarily to beat him at his own game, but they will never enable us to bring about genuine change. And this fact is only threatening to those women who still define the master's house as their only source of support. (Lorde, 1984, p. 111)

This offers some interesting insights to social psychology too. If we're serious about wanting meaningful change in our psychological paradigms, we need to not only step outside of the master's house to see the bigger picture, we need to tear it down, smash its windows, and set the whole thing alight. We cannot, as Lorde notes, attempt to re-build a psychology that continues to have foundations firmly within the 'the master's house'. Therefore, we need some pretty radical new ways of 'doing' psychology.

New methods for age-old questions

The problem, it seems, is that experimental methodologies may indeed be incompatible with a concern for social justice. Conducting experimental research typically goes something like this: researchers randomise participants to a condition, ask them to perform some kind of task or activity, and then they quantify the data and crunch the numbers to test whether their predictions hold true. The question of whether these kinds of approaches to social research are well equipped to deal with the deeply human and subjective concerns of social justice is a tricky one. There are two possible solutions here: we either dismantle the notion that there is only one correct way to research the human condition entirely, or we re-evaluate social psychology's concern for fairness and social equality entirely.

You might expect that the suggestion of abandoning, or at least reappraising, the core scientific method is likely to cause rifts among social psychologists. After all, the study of social psychology has been built on the idea that large-scale (woefully unethical – but that's another conversation) 'controlled' field studies are the best way to study real-world phenomena. You would be right!

Feminist questions require feminist research methods (*A Feminist Companion to Research Methods in Psychology* will address this – Capdevila & Frith, forthcoming). As Clarke and Braun have argued, feminist methodology should ultimately aim to centre women's voices and experience through means that are critical, creative, and innovative (Clarke & Braun, 2019; Jankowski, Braun, & Clarke, 2017). After all, the capacity for creativity is part of the fun of feminist psychology! There is a growing body of research that uses diverse and creative methodologies to ask feminist research questions (Gergen, 2008), with the aim of capturing feminist psychology's concern for *lived experience* of difference (Willig, 2017). On the back of this, feminist psychology has earned itself a reputation for being disruptive or 'socially transformative' (Wigginton & LaFrance, 2019), an idea that we rather like.

Feminist psychology typically centres and celebrates vulnerability, positionality, and reflexivity (Griffin, 2012). Reflexivity is a hallmark of all feminist research, referring to the process of critical self-reflection through which researchers consider their positionality and how it may impact the research process and outcomes (Braun & Clarke, 2019). Similarly, Rutherford (2007) prompts us to think carefully about not only the questions that we are asking of our psychological data, but also *who* is doing the research. This concern must also be applied to correction of the literature; if marginalised voices are not centred within the reappraisal process, the 'masculinist culture' of science will continue to persist.

NEW METHODS – PARTICIPATORY RESEARCH

As social psychology continually adapts and moulds itself around these new challenges, the way that we think about some of the core ideas of psychology must also change. For example, psychologists who work with children, either as researchers or in professional practice, must grapple with power relations that are asymmetrical – adults have the power, children do not. A feminist approach to this kind of work highlights that children have their own kind of expertise that is situated within their own lived experience (e.g. Oswell, 2013). As Langsted (1994) suggests, psychologists should make use of creative methodologies, such as photography and arts-based data collection, that centre and amplify children's voices in their own language. *Participatory research* (e.g. Participatory Action Research; Kemmis, 2006), which invites a collaborative, shared type of power and democratic decision-making, can break down some of the barriers to participation that often pervade more traditional social psychology research.

Feminist experiments

We have been rather critical of experimental work here, but it is also important to note that there are many wonderful examples of feminist research that uses quantitative, experimental methodologies. In fact, the divide between quantitative and qualitative research can lead to unhelpful distinctions in the pursuit of feminist research, which we are cautious about perpetuating. Some experimental work has done a huge amount of good for the feminist agenda, for example, feminist research has used Implicit Association Tasks to demonstrate the implicit gender biases that people hold (e.g. Bailey, LaFrance, & Dovidio, 2020). Research has also demonstrated how exposure to negative stereotypes can harm girls' quantitative performance, i.e. 'stereotype threat' theory (Tomasetto,

Alparone, & Cadinu, 2011). Therefore, while we advocate here for more interpretative, reflexive, co-created research, there is also great value in experimental work that stems from a feminist perspective. We like how Wigginton and Lafrance tackle this debate:

> ... one cannot claim that qualitative methods (e.g. semi-structured interviews) are inherently 'feminist', or that quantitative methods (e.g. survey measures) are 'unfeminist'. All methods can be used in sexist ways; and, conversely, all can be used toward feminist ends. (Wigginton & Lafrance, 2019, p. 11)

Achievements of feminist social psychologists

Historically, social psychology has been dominated by mainstream approaches to studying the human condition, which predominantly were concerned with minimising bias and continuing a façade of objective, scientific science. A more feminist approach to the study of social interaction has since challenged these assumptions. Over the years, feminist social psychologists have made progress, marked by a number of distinct achievements of the movement. Feminist social psychologists have, for example:

- acknowledged how knowledge and science are situated within *norms* that are inherently patriarchal, or 'male serving';
- studied the ways in which women, girls, and other marginalised groups are often positioned to be subordinate, with less agency and voice than other groups;
- adopted a more social constructionist view of the human condition, which considers how supposedly natural phenomena are actively socially constructed to have a particular meaning by the culture and society that it exists within;
- promoted the use of qualitative, participatory methods that destabilise some of the rigid ideas about who has expertise in a research context.

SECTION SUMMARY

- In this section, we have considered some meaty questions about the very nature of feminist methodologies in social psychology, paying particular attention to how feminist social psychology can offer new ways of 'doing' psychology through new methods.
- We have been introduced to some big concepts that will be important throughout the Companion (and indeed beyond!), such as reflexivity, intersectionality, and social constructionism.
- Feminist social psychology ultimately advocates for the meaningful and thoughtful inclusion of all people in social research, which can be achieved well with *participatory* methods.

ACTIVITY 2.3: A feminist social psychology to-do list

Throughout this chapter, we've seen that feminist social psychology made promising progress in the early days of its development. This progress signals an important shift in scientific culture, or the *paradigm* that psychological science exists within. However, as you might have guessed, there's plenty left to do!

Feminist social psychology can address inequalities, promote alternative ways of thinking about research, and invite a more critical and creative approach to the study of human beings. To get you thinking about how this agenda can tackle concerns of mainstream research, we now invite you to construct your own feminist social psychology 'to-do list'. The following prompts may help you to guide your to-do list:

- Given what we've discussed so far in this book, what concerns do you have for the interplay between feminist ideas and mainstream social psychology?
- What do you hope that feminist social psychology will also uncover, challenge, or promote?
- What should feminist social psychologists' priority be?
- What important work is still left to be done?

Ideally, you should keep this list and revisit it once you've finished reading this book. You can then (hopefully!) tick off some of the items from your list, as you learn more about how feminist social psychology has developed its agenda and activities. Having read the book, you should be left with a list of to-do's that have not been explicitly captured by the discipline so far, which is an ideal place for you to start your feminist killjoy journey!

Rethinking and re-evaluating the whole notion of psychology being a 'science' is a core issue within feminist thinking that we'll keep revisiting throughout the book. Despite a growing body of feminist research that rethinks how psychology and science fit together, the mainstream approach is one that continues to rely on principles of the scientific process. Mainstream psychological scientists generate hypotheses, think up robust ways of testing these research questions, collect or locate data, analyse the data, and report whether or not the original hypotheses were supported or not. In theory, it should be a neat, straightforward process.

CHAPTER SUMMARY

- We have discussed the interplay between feminist thinking and social psychology, outlining some of the shifts that happened within social psychology, in terms of how bias and 'the scientific method' are viewed.
- We have learned about reflexivity in social psychology, and how it acknowledges that as *social* beings, social psychologists can so easily build their own biases and limitations into how they conduct their research and develop their theories.
- We have thought about the future of feminist social psychology.

3 Gender, identity, and intersectionality

Learning objectives

Study of this chapter (including its activities) should enable you to:

- Know how social psychology started out as an exclusive 'private men's club' – established by its 'founding fathers', and just how patriarchal it was in its assumptions and view of the world.
- Recognise just how crucial the term 'gender' has been to the development of feminist social psychology.
- Know more about how the concept of 'gender' engendered a flourishing of theory and research in social psychology.
- Understand better what is meant by gender as a *performance* or action.
- Gain insight into how gender is produced, and how gendered identities are socially constructed, navigated, and negotiated.
- Describe four of the versions of 'the self' that have been recognised within social psychology, and give examples of how they intersect with gender.
- Explain what is meant more broadly by intersectionality, give illustrative examples, and explain why it is so important to feminist theorising.

Invisible women

As a feminist historian of science, Londa Shiebinger has pointed out that 'for nearly three hundred years the only permanent female presence at the Royal Society [The UK's National Academy of Science] was a skeleton preserved in the society's anatomical collection' (Shiebinger, 1991, p. 26). At its origins, psychology was an academic discipline operating as an exclusive 'private men's club' – where only gentlemen were allowed to join, devoting their time to writing for and talking to each other about *man*ly things and working together on *man*ly pursuits.

ELITE GENTLEMEN'S CLUBS

Britain has a history of setting up exclusive clubs for gentlemen. Many now accept women as members, but others, such as the Garrick Club in London, remain exclusively 'gentlemen's clubs', with women excluded. In 2020, a group of women got together to challenge this, arguing that many of the Garrick Club's members are senior lawyers – and this exclusion is part of the reason for the massive and continuing gender inequalities in the legal profession.

It's hardly surprising, then, that the 'founding fathers' of social psychology perceived the world through finely attuned and thoroughly patriarchal male 'ways of seeing' (called the *'male gaze'*). It was a vision of psychology in which women were regarded as neither interesting nor important. As you saw in Chapter 2, Muzafer Sherif was interested in developing theories about 'intergroup conflict', yet he genuinely believed that only what went on between groups of men or of boys really mattered. Fixated on their own *worldview*, these early – male – social psychologists did however start researching women, but only in ways that served their male interests. They weren't interested in what women did or thought, but instead what makes women attractive to men. With hindsight this looks more like a bunch of cis white blokes 'checking out the babes' than any kind of rigorous research. Early social psychologists' assumptions and behaviour were simply compliant with the operating rules within the mainstream (sometimes ironically called *malestream*) culture of universities at the time.

By the 1950s and 1960s, psychology departments did gradually take in more female students and, ultimately, appointed a few women as junior staff. Women's opinions began to be heard and, importantly, to influence what went on. Their challenges led social psychologists to become more aware of their own biases and preconceptions, and more willing to acknowledge, say, the limitations and distortions created through operating within a patriarchal worldview. It is worth noting that more recently social psychologists have also begun to address the impact of psychology's colonising/imperialistic knowledge-base.

When and why 'gender' became important

Rhoda Unger was certainly not the first woman to question psychology's almost total preoccupation with biology and evolution as explanations for social phenomena such as selfhood. There is a whole raft of women psychologists whose work has effectively been 'lost' because of the hurdles they faced in getting published. But by getting her article about the difference between sex and gender into the prestigious and popular science magazine *American Psychologist* (1979), Unger made people (including social psychologists) sit up and take notice. In particular, it opened the way for social psychologists to write and speak about – and make sense of – why women appeared to be so different from men. By offering them the word 'gender' as a distinctly different concept from 'sex', she provided social psychologists (especially those of a feminist bent) with the means by which they could make evident the profound and wide-ranging psychological, societal, and cultural forces (and power-plays) that contribute to creating and maintaining maleness and femaleness. Seldom used in the 1950s and 1960s, by the 1970s the word 'gender' was rapidly taken up, not just in the social sciences but also within popular culture more generally. In this way, it became part of 'what everybody knows' – it was literally a changer of hearts and minds.

Opening up social psychology

Crucially, the concept of gender created ways for feminists to theorise about the subtleties and nuances of, say, social interaction between men and women, and it changed what social psychology could do. Increasing attention got paid to the many and complex ways in which social and cultural expectations, different values about the upbringing of children, social rules about conduct, and so on, play such a big part in what it means to be a boy or girl, a woman or a man. This led social psychology away from basing its theories on biological differences to ones exploring the impact of, for example, gendered social norms; and the role played by social interaction in the development of gender roles and gender identities.

Note, too, the difference between where agency is located in the two forms of explanation. Biological processes are not generally under a person's control, and we are often unaware of them operating. But using the term 'gender' acknowledges the profoundly *psycho-socio-cultural* nature of being male, female, or, say, non-binary. The conceptual move is from the fixedness of a mechanistic biological entity, delimited by genetics, to the fluidity and intentionality of a profoundly *social* being who constantly changes and adapts, who possesses ambitions and passions, and who seeks to determine the kind of life they live as well as the person they are. Some early social psychologists such as William James conceived of humankind in much this way – as active, adaptable, self-determining, and self-aware, recognising the complex and sophisticated beings that humans are. This is not to say we can freely choose. Society can lock us up in mental straightjackets as much as, or more than, anything to do with our embodiment. But some of us are now moving into an era where there is at least the potential to self-identify ourselves as something else entirely.

Academic life as a social system

The message here is that academic life is itself a social system, which, as it changes, has a profound influence on, for example, which topics are popular and what kinds of assumptions are built into theories, and hence what kinds of research get done. A feminist perspective on psychology only became possible when the world outside of the academy provided the conditions that would allow it to flourish. You can get a sense of this by listening to Carol Gilligan's story of how she came to recognise that men and women speak 'in a different voice'. She recounts how she worked (as a lowly assistant) for two of the 'Big Men' in psychology, Erik Erikson and Lawrence Kohlberg, both of whom theorised on the moral development of children, basing their research on all-boy samples. She describes the impact of realising that that was the case, which was, she says, 'like an epiphany!'

See and hear for yourself

Visit the Feminist Voices Project (www.feministvoices.com) to locate the interview with Carol Gilligan: 'Changing the Voice of the Conversation'. You will find it in the Feminist Presence section. She speaks about how she came to write her book *In a Different Voice* (1993), and how she experienced the major turning point in social psychology going on at the time.

Gender gets *done*

Another major conceptual shift came in the 1970s when Candice West and Don Zimmerman began to examine in detail the interplay of conversations between men and women and observed some very striking stuff. They counted conversational features like the number of times men and women interrupted and talked over each other, and found highly significant differences. Almost always, it was men who interrupted women, talked over them, and simply dominated the conversation (Zimmerman and West, 1975; West and Zimmerman, 1977). They spent the next ten years seeking to get these findings published in any of the 'big' journals around at the time. It took until 1987 for their paper on 'Doing gender' to get the public recognition it deserved. In it they proposed a radical idea – that gender is not something that you 'are', but something that you do! As Judith Butler (1993) rather more famously argued, gender is here seen as *performative*. We particularly like the way Deborah Cameron puts it: 'gender is not a "thing" but a process, and one which is never finished' – something people 'do' or 'perform' as opposed to something they have (1998, p. 16).

In their 1987 paper, West and Zimmerman made their reading of the distinction between sex and gender very clear. They defined *sex* as a 'determination made through the application of socially agreed-upon biological criteria for classifying persons as male or female' (p. 127) – in other words, a category judgement. In everyday life, they note that people don't (usually) go around checking each other's genitals, but rely on observing the 'normative conceptions of attitudes and activities appropriate for one's sex category' (p. 127). By contrast, *gender*, they say, is a matter of 'managing *situated* conduct' in relation to how people expect men and women to act. This is not a matter of categorisation but rather one of social control – what Nikolas Rose calls 'governing the soul' and Michel Foucault refers to as the 'technology of the self'. Both theorists propose that people's identities – including their gender identities – are not hard-wired in the brain but constructed and, indeed, regulated by social, psychological, and cultural forces. We will look at these ideas later in the chapter.

Even today it is hard for people to shake off the assumption that 'naturally, boys will be boys', or 'little girls are made of "sugar and spice and all things nice"'. This has not been helped by the way many social psychologists accept the advantages of the concept of gender and adopt it in their theorising – as in gender roles, gender schema, and gender identities – yet still retain the conviction that gender operates at the *individual* level. West and Zimmerman contest this explicitly: 'gender is … the product of *social doings of some sort*' (1987, p. 129, our emphasis). Moreover, 'it is constituted through interaction'. In other words, it is a social *phenomenon*, manifested through the way people behave towards each other. Moreover, it really matters in relation to, say, sex stereotyping – this is not something that happens in the 'nooks and crannies' of interactions, but is constantly being woven into the very fabric of our everyday sayings and doings. Bev Skeggs (2005) showed this delightfully in her observations of the banter between the 'vulgar hen party babes' who invaded the louche gay men's elegant Velvet Lounge spaces in Manchester.

Since social psychologists began to look at gender, they have been much more able to explore the ways in which women fare badly in a world that is still largely man-made (the previous example not withstanding). Feminists have made good use of empirical data to fight for more equitable treatment in terms of salaries, promotion prospects, legal protections, access to sport facilities, and competition prizes. They have fared less well in areas like access to appropriate health care, safety in terms of car design, voice recognition and AI more generally – *Siri* as originally designed could help you with finding a sex worker but not an abortion clinic! Things have moved on a bit since then, but generally we still live in a world that is designed for men (Perez, 2019). Do, if you can, read Caroline Criado-Perez's article in the *Guardian* (2019) – like most people, you may have no idea of the far greater risks that women face, in areas ranging from car design to knife crime, since neither car seats nor body armour fit the average woman. Most people are surprised by the amount and severity of the risks women run by living in a man-made world.

SECTION SUMMARY

- The concept of gender gave social psychologists a way to challenge the discipline's preoccupation with biology, and got them exploring the multiple ways in which social norms, religious mores, and children's upbringing were involved in creating female and male identities.
- From some perspectives, gender is not a set of traits or roles or a variable – it is *performed*, within social interactions.
- Statistics on gender differences can be helpful in identifying gender inequalities.
- A lot of gender differences are, however, hidden – within a world that still tends to be designed by men *for* men, with little concern about the needs and entitlements of women.

Gender, self, and identity

Since its inception, social psychology has always been fascinated with the self – the nature of personhood, what we would now refer to as a person's identity. Social psychologists generally recognise three 'Founding Fathers' of theory in this field. William James (1907), one of the earliest social psychologists, identified two different forms of selfhood: the 'me' – the self-as-known-by-others; and the 'I' – the self-as-known by me. George Herbert Mead, a sociologist, took up James' ideas and expanded on them (Mead, 1934). Mead's main concern was to reconcile what went on in individual minds with what goes on socially among people. This interest in the interplay between the individual and the social continues to this day in theorisation about identities – if anything, it has become more important. Finally, there was Irving Goffman, another sociologist, who drew attention to the way that everyday life is mostly about interaction *between* people as they play out the 'drama of life'.

The self in experimental social psychology

In the 1960s and 1970s, when psychology came to be seen as 'the science of human behaviour', social psychologists took to calling themselves 'experimental social psychologists'. In this context, selfhood became seen in essentialist terms – using concepts like 'personality traits' and theories on how humans go through a series of natural cognitive transitions from infant to fully-formed adult. Much effort was put into studying, for example, how children acquire their sense of their own gender, through processes like imitation and the influence of role models.

The self in critical social psychology

In the 1980s and 1990s, a number of social psychologists became disenchanted with experimentation, and the early work of James, Mead, and Goffman became popular once more. Social psychologists came to be more interested in the social processes involved in moulding and shaping how people make sense of themselves, who they are, and more generally what being a person means and signifies. It was also recognised that there was no simple, universal way of being a self. Personhood varies by historical time and geographical place, in relation to the local values and assumptions within different cultures and communities. These days, as steps are taken to **decolonise** psychology, White and privileged social psychologists are gradually recognising that the Western preoccupation with individualism, for instance, is by no means universal. This has led to a recognition that, in a global context, identity operates mainly in relation to others and often on the basis of connectedness within groups and communities.

Governing the soul

For critical social psychologists, adopting this new paradigm led to theory-making becoming a lot more suspicious. There was a shift from seeing selves as *influenced* by social processes to being *governed* by those in power. Maybe the strongest advocate of this perspective is the sociologist, Nikolas Rose, whose book *Governing the Soul* hit social psychology in 1989. In it he argued that power is constantly being covertly exercised – in particular by what he calls the '**psy complex**', made up of psychology, psychiatry, and psychother-apy – in ways that impose control on anyone who deviates from the normal – a society's expectations and requirements of its citizens.

Similar ideas were expressed somewhat earlier by Michel Foucault, a French theorist working in psychology. In his book *Discipline and Punish* (published in France in 1975 and translated into English in 1977), Foucault describes in detail the 'dense networks of power' that, he argued, permeate our relation-ships with each other. He used the term 'the micro-politics of power' to describe what is going on in every human interaction, from the institutional to the highly intimate. Foucault gave feminists one of the most useful terms when thinking about identity: *subject positioning*. By this he drew attention to the ways in which many aspects of our identities are predetermined by how we are posi-tioned – as a woman, as a wife, as Black.

These identities vary over time and location. A good example is the classic film *The French Lieutenant's Woman* (well worth downloading if you missed it – it's a very clever film). In it the narrative keeps shifting, juxtaposing between the main storyline portraying how a woman loses her 'good name' by having an affair with the French Lieutenant, and a contemporary version where the actress has an affair with the actor concerned. In both cases, a woman and a man have 'illicit' sex, but the consequences are very different for the woman. In the historical story, she is rejected by 'good society'; in the contemporary ver-sion, in contrast, the actor playing the female role provokes a little gentle tutting but would never be socially ostracised. She would never be identified as a 'fallen woman', utterly excluded from 'polite society'.

Changing the subject

In the 1980s and 1990s, in response to mounting criticism of experimental social psychology, for a growing fringe group (critical psychologists) theorisation in social psychology underwent considerable change, especially in the way psy-chologists understood personhood. Out went the mechanistic models of the 1960s and 1970s and in came (for some) much more sophisticated theories about what we now call 'identity'. In 1984, a radical new book by Henriques et al. titled *Changing the Subject* really shook things up. In it the authors argued for a radical overhaul of social psychology's view of itself and of *the* self. Its explicit agenda was, literally, to change the conception of both 'the subject' *of* psychology and 'the subject' *in* psychology – 'to demonstrate that the individ-ual is not a fixed or given entity, but rather a particular product of historically specific practices of social regulation' (Henriques et al., 1984, p. 12).

Gender identity

The term 'gender identity' has become very popular – Google it and see the range of results it creates, from the magazine *Cosmopolitan* to sites on safe-guarding children. It all sounds a bit competitive – long lists of terms you need to know, understand, and use to 'pass' as culturally aware. As societies open up to a wide variety of intersections between genders, identity has become much more difficult to pin down.

ACTIVITY 3.1

Let's get started by considering four different versions of the self (loosely based around Wetherell and Maybin, 1996):

- A **personal self**, sometimes called an individual self, which regards people as autonomous, self-contained, and self-reliant; entitled and encouraged to pursue their own concerns, motives, aspirations, and desires. Its overt goals focus on **empowering** individuals to be the best they can be – having high self-esteem and high self-efficacy.
- A **social self**, introduced by *social identity* theory, which views selfhood as a product of belonging to a particular social group, moulded by social processes (such as socialisation and identification) and by social influences (such as the kind of upbringing a person receives). It stresses the importance of the bonding engendered through social life and social relationships.
- A **relational self**, which regards one's identity as inexorably integrated with others, in terms of mutual duties and obligations, deference and authority, and one's responsibilities to one's family, friendship network, and community. It tends to be dominant within **majority world** societies that focus on family obligations and value connectedness and mutual support. Hamaguchi (1985), for instance, points out that in Japan, a highly collectivist culture, the word for self, *jibun*, means 'one's portion of the shared space'.
- A **positioned self**, drawn from Foucault's theories about how power is exercised within social relationships – the micro-politics of power – and by social control. It also draws upon Rose's ideas about 'governing the soul', the way that institutions like the 'psy complex' provide those in power with the means to regulate the identities that are available – such as the damaged identity that is associated with mental illness.

Take some time to get your head around the four different versions of identity, then think about how each implies different things for men and women. If working on your own, make lists for each version of what are the variants for male and female identities. For example, think about how the individual self will work out for a man and then for a woman. You can run this as a group activity by splitting into four groups, each one concentrating on one of the versions for 10–15 minutes. Then open a general discussion, to come to some conclusions. Alternatively as a group, you can do some exploring beforehand, looking at what recent social psychology research has to offer us.

Gendered identities

Here are some insights from feminist social psychology research as to the ways in which identities are gendered:

Gendering the individual self

This very *individualised* version of identity is generally seen as 'macho' or even 'alpha male'. It is firmly based on notions of male superiority (Saini, 2019) and entitlement, as well as encouraging men to be highly competitive. The female version is much less of a cosy and comfortable fit. Ros Gill and her colleagues have done a fair amount of research around the ways in which, under *neoliberalism*, women, in particular, are under pressure to demonstrate they can be 'resilient' when life gets tough. They need to rely on themselves. Together with Shani Orgad, for example, Gill explored how magazines, self-help books, and smartphone apps promoting positive mental attitudes (PMA) are marketed to middle-class young women as ways of being successful as a woman. By constantly extolling young women to 'Go confidently in the direction of your dreams' (and lots of other stuff like that), these apps exert relentless pressure to be 'bounce-backable' and resilient (Gill & Orgad, 2018).

Gendering the social self

It is important to recognise how gender stereotypes and norms harm boys and men too (we'll come to the definitions of gender stereotypes in Chapter 7). Jennifer Bosson and Joseph Vandello have highlighted how masculinity or manhood is socially constructed as something that is elusive, and must be fought for, proven, and earned by men. Their 'precarious manhood theory' (Vandello et al., 2008) posits that masculinity is constantly 'under threat' in a way that femininity is not. Therefore, men experience pressure to perform their masculinity correctly, thus leading to aggression and frustration (see Bosson & Vandello, 2011). This means that life is particularly difficult for men whose sense of masculinity falls outside of the rigid mandates of social norms of manhood. Research has demonstrated this in many different social contexts. Ann Phoenix's research into the anti-swot culture among teenage schoolboys in London is a great example. She and her colleagues showed that, in school, boys need to negotiate their identities in ways that allow them to defend their masculinity while still making enough progress in their schoolwork to gain the qualifications needed to get a good job (Phoenix, Frosh, & Pattman, 2003). To be seen as a 'swot' is far too feminine a thing to admit to. This accommodation proves particularly hard for Black boys, which severely limits their job prospects. Asian boys find it less difficult, as they are not expected to be as 'hard' as the Black boys. Girls tend to fare better and in the minority world and now outnumber boys in higher education. But ever more demanding expectations – especially about their gendered roles as mothers – kick in later. We will explore the social role of mothering in more detail in Chapter 8.

Gendering the relational self

One context in which we see differences in attitudes and expectations between men and women is in relation to caregiving. Carol Gilligan (1993) identified caring as the moral ideal for women (as opposed to the way men value abstract values such as justice and morality). She explains that for women, 'the ideal of care is ... an activity of relationship, of seeing and responding to need, taking care of the world by sustaining the web of connection so no one is left alone' (Gilligan, 1993, p. 62). This applies to both care within families and that by professional carers. In a quest to establish a theory of women's caring, Judith Wuest noted that it is 'a complex reality that is poorly understood' (2001, p. 168). The women who do it view it as burdensome and stressful, yet fulfilling, satisfying, and life-enhancing. Moreover, it is not a choice but, according to feminist scholars, comes about through material and ideological forces. Wuest notes that these days in the minority world there are growing expectations for female relatives to take on caring responsibilities, because:

1 There has been a feminisation of the labour force, where women form the majority of paid carers, employed in low-status jobs on zero-hour contracts, low paid and in non-unionised roles, with limited career prospects.

2 There has been a dramatic shift in health and social care policies within the minority world, where a commitment to a welfare state has been besieged by the neoliberal values of a powerful market economy. This has disproportionally impacted on women. Care that used to be provided by professionals has been increasingly off-loaded onto families – which generally means that the female relatives are persuaded to take it on.

3 Health care policy has itself seen its own shift from providing acute care to a preoccupation with prevention and healthy living lifestyles – where, once again, it is predominantly women who are held responsible.

4 All of these demands are exacerbated within an ageing population, where women are being expected to take on the care of their elderly relatives, with the same fervour as they care for children. Indeed, many women are trying to cope with the impact of their own menopause, while caring for their teenage children *and* elderly relatives at the same time!

Gendering the positional self

A good example of the gendered positional self is where a person gets *situationally* stereotyped – by becoming a stepmother, for instance. An illustration of this is provided by Sandra Roper and Rose Capdevila, who showed how stepmothers seek to avoid being socially positioned as wicked and cruel and/or as 'gold diggers' (2020, p. 248). As the authors state, stepmothers have implicitly acquired **'troubled identities'** that they must work to salvage if they are to acquire the authenticity of being a 'good woman'. The authors used a narrative approach to identify the strategies that stepmothers use to avoid being lumbered with a damaged identity, exploring the discursive resources they use to redeem themselves.

In this context, stepmothers occupy a precarious position, and so they need to do a lot of 'identity repair'. Roper and Capdevila identify three main **discourses** through which stepmothers were able to do this repair work:

- by 'rescuing' the man concerned – for example, by providing a home for his children and paying the mortgage and bills, making her a financial asset rather than a gold-digger;
- by ameliorating the stigma of fathers who are seen as having abandoned their children – for example, by advising them on how to get on better with the children's mother;
- by blaming the ex-wife (or the grandmother) for the damage done to the father and his children as a result of their split, and presenting herself as having a greater capacity to repair the family situation.

Another good example of positioning being resisted is associated with the **Missy** identity (Kim, 2011). This is a recently constructed female identity from South Korea, where the expected identity of a married woman is to become a modest, retiring, and somewhat frumpy wife and mother. Becoming a 'Missy' instead – a progressive, modern, and stylish woman, free to follow fashion and to progress her own life opportunities – allows wives to resist the boring stereotype traditionally imposed on them. The Missy identity was created initially through advertising, as a way to encourage women to buy more. Now, though, it is being promoted by women themselves. We include it as an example of the way social change alters the kinds of identity that can be claimed.

SECTION SUMMARY

- Since its inception, social psychology has always been interested in the self – both the self-as-others-know-us and the self-as-we-know-ourselves.
- Critical social psychology recognises four main versions of the self: the individual self, the social self, the relational self, and the positioned self.
- Cultures and societies vary in which one of these versions is most dominant. Broadly, the *individual self* aligns best with US and UK values; the *social self* with European values; and the *relational self* with Eastern ways of thinking, prevalent in Asia, Japan, and China. But it's not that simple, since the *positioned self* is not easily located – and most of us can relate to all four selves in different contexts and circumstances.
- Each conceptual system has its own specific engagements with gender – but all make a strong distinction between what are considered acceptable masculine and feminine identities.
- These introduce us to the ways in which people do identity work – they seek to repair the damage of having a 'spoiled' identity, for example. Examples include identity work to resist the stereotypes of 'wicked stepmothers' and 'boring housewives'.

Intersectionality

You may have noticed how, in Phoenix's research into 'anti-swot' culture among schoolboys, what went on tended to intersect the performance of masculine gender with 'race' (the quotation marks indicate we recognise this is a distinctly dodgy term). In that study, Phoenix and her colleagues identified three groups – White boys, Black boys (of African Caribbean heritage), and Asian boys. They noted that 'Black, White and Asian boys were considered to be differently positioned in terms of hegemonic masculinity' (Phoenix et al., 2003, p. 240).

Phoenix argues that masculinity is particularly difficult for Black boys to negotiate, in that Black boys are *expected* to be aggressively masculine and troublesome, a positioning that is very hard to shake off. Majors and Billston (1992) found that, in the USA, African American boys gain popularity among their peers because they come across as powerful and willing to talk back at their teachers – but this comes at a cost. 'Black young men find themselves constrained with in a construction of masculinity that gives them power. However, it contributes to their relative lack of power in society as a whole' (Phoenix et al., 2003, p. 240). Social psychologists – particularly feminists scholars – are increasingly coming to recognise that gender identities are never simple or homogeneous but are always shot through with elements of other social identities, such as 'race' (skin colour), ethnic heritage, social class, disability, and sexual orientation. Thus, any attempt to compare males and females without taking into account these other identities will lead to overly broad generalisations that might be totally inaccurate.

It started as a legal term

The word **intersectionality** began as a legal term, adopted by Kimberlé Crenshaw, a Black female lawyer (now a professor) in the USA, to draw attention to the way that employees who are both women and Black are often discriminated against more toughly because of the 'double whammy' of being both Black and a woman. Manufacturing companies had, historically, had different recruitment regulations for different genders. For example, in a case against General Motors, where Black women had not been employed before 1964, all the Black women employees were laid off in a seniority-based policy decision during a recession, in a way White women who had worked there longer were not. Crenshaw used the term in making her case against the judge's dismissal of their claim.

Career progression

The compounding of negative attributions more generally has a real impact on Black women's career advancement and chances of promotion. As an example, let us look at the overall figures for Black professors. In the UK, the latest figures indicate that there are just 85 Black professors in the whole of its higher education sector. This represents just 0.6% of the total number of professors; and of all Black academics, only 4.6% of them achieve a professorship, compared with 11.2% of White academics (Advance HE, 2018). Overall, White academics are approximately three times more likely to be successful when applying for a professorship compared with their peers from Black and minority ethnic backgrounds (UCU, 2012).

When we look at intersectionality in terms of Black women professors in the UK, in 2019 there were only twenty-five of them. A really good place to find out more is a report funded by the University College Union (UCU) entitled *Staying Power: The Career Experiences and Strategies of Black Female Professors*, written by Nicola Rollock (2019). This is a very clear and informative read. A Black academic herself, Rollock reports on interviews she conducted with twenty of the twenty-five professors identified. Their descriptions spell out in painful detail how hard they have had to strive to gain their title, and, despite the status it endows, how they are still often treated as the *'mules and donkeys'* of the workforce (Rollock, 2019, p. 4). Increasingly, social psychology is being forced to face up to its institutional racism, and needs to take steps to overcome its stereotyping of the people it studies.

SECTION SUMMARY

- Intersectionality is where an identity is formed around two or more forms of disadvantage/oppression, which, when brought together, can exacerbate the degree of 'Otherness' so that the person faces even more hostility and antagonism. As an example, young working-class women are often viewed as feckless, especially when they get a bit drunk. Contrast this with mature, middle-class men who are perceived merely as *'bon viveurs* having a good time' (Day, Gough, & McFadden, 2004).

- Such positioning can cause all sorts of harm, from poor prospects in employment, through being relentlessly bullied, to being subjected to powerful regulation, including requirements to maintain self-control. It can also be manifested through being ignored and forgotten.

- For feminists, intersectionality is crucially important, as it raises issues of entitlement and of who can legitimately 'speak for' others.

This chapter has been a bit of a whistle-stop journey through social psychology's theoretical shifts and changes, especially in relation to changing ideas about selfhood and identity. Our aim has been to expand your knowledge and understanding of the role played by feminist social psychologists. If you want to find out more, we particularly recommend you read Nicola Rollock's (2019) account of what it is like to be a Black professor in HE in Britain. As White women ourselves, we were pretty shocked, but very glad to improve our understanding of Black Lives Matter and what academics need to do to fight the institutional racism that remains pervasive in British universities.

CHAPTER SUMMARY

- Feminist social psychology had an uneasy start, at a time when it was dominated by patriarchy and it was assumed that men and women were biologically quite different creatures.

- By championing the concept of gender, early feminists challenged this perception, drawing attention to other reasons for differences such as cultural expectations and social processes, including different goals in the raising of boys and girls.

- Many feminist social psychologists, such as Carol Gilligan, worked first as assistants to the 'Big Men' who created modern social psychology. Their feminism grew out of their realisation that, as women, they saw things very differently from the way their bosses did.

- Gradually, as more women studied and worked in social psychology, they came up with different theories, different ways of doing research, and different ethical principles.

- Societies and cultures vary in the way they understand selfhood: some see selves as individuals, some in terms of belonging to particular social groups, and some in terms of their relationships with and obligations to others.

4 | Social psychology's horrible history

Learning objectives

Study of this chapter (including its activities) should enable you to:

- Recognise that feminism is not anti-men but anti-patriarchy.
- Describe what patriarchy means and summarise the harms it does to women and to men.
- Get a handle on the way that women were, historically, excluded from academic life, and why they are still underrepresented in its hierarchies.
- Outline a brief history of the key women pioneers, mainly those in the USA and UK who, within social psychology, led the challenge to this misogyny.
- Find out more about the history of feminist psychology where you live and operate.
- Describe and explain the key issues around sexual violence, including sexual harassment.
- Find out about how, historically, social psychology schools and departments positioned women students and colleagues as 'fair game' for sexual exploitation.
- Know more about how social psychologists conducted experiments that were essentially forms of sexual harassment.
- Gain knowledge of the legal changes that have been made to address these forms of mistreatment and the systematic improvements being made to make academia a more woman-friendly place to study and work.
- Get a good sense of how far these changes have been effective, and just how much patriarchal beliefs and expectations persist to this day.
- Begin to develop the knowledge and skills necessary for resistance, and how to act together with other feminists to make academia more welcoming to, and respectful of, all groups who fall out of the hegemonic male (or default male, or 'bro') category.

Patriarchy, 'bro' culture, and hegemonic masculinity

Patriarchy's mistreatment of women and others is primarily about how individuals and groups behave, not about gender itself. A recent – but very useful – term to describe what is involved is *'bro'* – used in the US to indicate a certain kind of predominantly male behaviour. (*Note*: This is a very White and privileged version of 'bro' – not the one adopted within Black male communities where it is a term of affection, meaning 'my brother' in a broad sense.) The following extract is from an article in *The Psychologist* that describes what being a 'bro' entails:

> Let's get the clichés out of the way: not all men are bros, and not all bros are men. 'Bro' does not refer to half of the world's population. There are similar neologisms with the same prefix: brocialism, socialism that ignores gendered oppression; broscience, unfounded fitness advice; and the prevalence of brogrammers in the technology industry (Chang, 2018). In all contexts, bros are identified by their behaviour and attitude, not their gender
>
> … a bro will often be condescending, forthright, aggressive, overpowering, and lacking kindness and self-awareness (Reagle, 2013). Although they solicit debate on important issues, they tend to resist descriptions of the complexities, nuances, and multiple perspectives on their argument. They often veer into antisocial patterns of dialogue, such as **sealioning**, the act of intruding on and trying to derail a conversation with disingenuous questions (Kirkham, 2017). You've interacted with a bro if you've ever had the feeling that what they're saying makes sense superficially but would be hard to implement in your own research practices. In general, bros find it hard to understand – or accept – that others will have a different lived experience. (Whitaker & Guest, 2020)

Patriarchy

Patriarchy. How passé. How 'yesterday'.
— Cynthia Enloe, 2017, p. 15

As Cynthia Enloe remarks in her book about patriarchy, *The Big Push* (2017), talking about patriarchy has become *so embarrassing*. Yet it is an embarrassment we're willing to endure, since we regard patriarchy as an essential concept for understanding gender relations. Enloe argues that the fact that it *is* so difficult for us to talk about it is to experience patriarchy at its most powerful. The social processes, assumptions, and pressures that are the basis of patriarchy are what allow it to prevail today and even flourish. By making patriarchy a word that many women have become too embarrassed to use (because it turns us into hairy, hot-blooded harridans), we deprive ourselves of a language and a powerful set of ideas that are essential for challenging this system and its distorted and misguided assumptions about gender that continue to undermine women's self-respect, self-confidence, and life-opportunities.

As we made clear in our myth-busting in Chapter 1, feminists do not see patriarchy as a deliberately malignant male conspiracy being waged against women. What we object to are the ways in which men, in acting out **hegemonic masculinity**, create toxic environments where men can easily misuse their power, especially over women. Both men and women can be harmed, constrained, and ostracised by patriarchal power. Feminists recognise that patriarchy is an ideological product of human history. Another way to describe patriarchy is as the kind of 'groupthink' that is fostered in a relatively isolated collective, such as an elite, expensive school that is specifically designed and run in order to transmit privilege from one generation to another and actively seeks to develop a sense of entitlement and superiority in its pupils.

This may best be understood by acknowledging that patriarchy is a form of social organisation; it is a system that describes how a person's gender presentation brings with it certain social roles, or a particular social standing, that does not accurately reflect their skill, credit, or ability. People who are understood by society to be men are given more social standing, and are assumed to be more deserving of power and status, than people who present as women. Importantly, when these *patriarchal* expectations are internalised, they can form part of a **worldview** or 'sense of self'. The idea that the world as we know it is fundamentally 'male-serving' becomes a default way of seeing things. Anything that challenges this dominant worldview (enter: feminist psychology!) is seen as problematic and threatening. For example, students often rate male lecturers as more helpful because they already assume female lecturers will be helpful and so don't see it as 'extra', which further reinforces the gender bias.

Taking a step away from social psychology for a moment, the original notion of patriarchy ultimately derives from the idea that the father is the 'head of the family'. After all, the word itself comes from the Greek *patriarkhēs*, which means 'ruling father'! It is where the position of head of the family is passed down through the male line alone. Patriarchal systems are unjust hierarchies which position men as superior and women as 'less than' or Other. The assumption that women should be subservient to men goes a long way back. Historically, the laws in many countries were framed in a very patriarchal way and remnants of this remain. For example, in Britain it wasn't until the introduction of the Married Women's Property Act of 1882 that married women were allowed to own their own property. Before then, women were legally subservient to their husbands. Once married, husband and wife became one person and any property (including such things as copyright) that the wife owned on her marriage automatically became the property of her husband, and her legal identity effectively ceased to exist.

Importantly, given the existence of patriarchal systems, this also means that there are whole *institutions* where patriarchy is deeply embedded in their culture, history, and heritage. Some schools and hospitals are patriarchal to the core; they endorse, reinforce, and reproduce unjust power relations between boys and girls, men and women, often in ways that weren't noticed until pesky feminists started making such a fuss. For example, research shows how women doctors and teachers continue to be paid less than their male counterparts on average, take on more pastoral roles that aren't valued or rewarded by promotion or career development, and are often evaluated by their appearance in appraisals and evaluations in a way that men aren't. Social psychology, historically, operated in a stoutly patriarchal system. This is evident from our new-found understanding of the Sherifs: the struggles that Carolyn Sherif faced were largely a result of her gender. There was never such a neat example of the power of patriarchy.

Default Man

One of the most accessible accounts of how patriarchy harms men is a book by the British artist, Grayson Perry – *The Descent of Man* (2017). Artistic, working class, and a transvestite, he regards himself as singularly capable of critically engaging with patriarchy. He sees it as coming from the immense sense of entitlement that elite men have as a birth-right, beguiling them into a whole range of **unconscious biases** – a tribe he calls **Default Man**. He observes that 'centuries of patriarchy have fashioned the world to reflect and favour the middle-class masculine viewpoint' (Perry, 2017, p. 35). It is another way of describing hegemonic masculinity; that is, men seeing themselves as naturally given superior power, influence, and entitlement. Perry describes in some detail how the 'straightjacket of the Default Man identity' is not one that works for members of other 'tribes'. Many men struggle, he says, with the demands of being an alpha male, with, for instance, the exaggerated heterosexuality required to become a 'stud' or a sexual predator. The powerful macho image of masculinity promoted by patriarchy makes men vulnerable to taking risks – to 'live hard and die young'– leading to a significantly lower life expectancy compared with women.

Hegemonic masculinity

This macho image is called **hegemonic masculinity**, and it' makes low-status men very vulnerable. This was recognised recently by the American Psychological Association (APA) issuing new clinical guidelines for working with boys and men, in which they state that a masculinity characterised by aggression, dominance, and emotional repression is harmful and should not be the basis for therapy. The APA also links 'macho' beliefs and attitudes to a higher rate of suicides among men, and men's reluctance to seek medical advice.

There is plenty of evidence of the way hegemonic masculinity makes life difficult for men if they deviate from the norm – by, for example, pursuing a female-dominated career such as nursing (Pullen & Simpson, 2009) or getting into a relationship with a woman who earns more than he does (Hettinger, Hutchinson, & Bosson, 2014). Broadly, the hegemonic masculinity **discourses** that pervade contemporary society mean that men face real threats to their masculine identity in gender non-conforming fields (Cross & Bagilhole, 2002; Bagilhole & Cross, 2006), and are therefore prompted to redefine their masculinity and its relationship with their chosen field (McDonald, 2013). Even proud heroes can get drawn in. The

Invictus Games is a good example, where wounded military veterans compete against each other to show how courageous they are. This can work well while they are still young, but becomes a real problem in old age.

SECTION SUMMARY

- Patriarchy is an historical product, a system of thought and action whereby highly privileged 'default men' are able to exercise their elite power to foster their own interests. Such men act out hegemonic masculinity in its very macho way of being male.
- In today's world, a new term for hegemonic masculinity is a bro – a person who is 'condescending, forthright, aggressive, overpowering, and lacking kindness and self-awareness' (Whitaker & Guest, 2020).
- Bros acting out hegemonic masculinity portray men as all-powerful, strong, and entitled. This masculine identity not only undermines women, but also men who are in any way unconventional.

Women's blighted careers

Historically, patriarchy has had a massive impact on universities – mostly set up by the Church and other exclusively male institutions, they were created in the same mould. Distrusted and not being seen as 'fully human', women were generally prohibited from campus other than as servants. Wood Sherif was absolutely not the only woman who had tremendous difficulty in building her career as a social psychologist. This section offers you the opportunity to get a sense of the barriers they had to face by looking at the stories of six other women aspiring to be a social psychologist. Our aim here is to look at the impact of trying to fit into a grimly hostile environment, having to fight constant battles, and to behave in certain ways to be taken seriously.

See and hear for yourself

Use the link to the Psychology's Feminist Voices website (www.feministvoices. com) to find the stories of: Mary Whiton Calkins, Mary Crawford, and Naomi Weisstein from the USA; and those of Sue Wilkinson, Celia Kitzinger, and Wendy Hollway from the UK.

Another excellent resource is a collection of writings by and about women by Mary Crawford and Rhoda Unger. Its first edition was called *In Our Own Words: Readings on the Psychology of Women and Gender* published by the Open University Press in 1997. It contains a number of first-hand accounts of the travails of early feminist psychologists, and papers written by feminist scholars about them. Much easier to get hold of is its second edition, published in 2000. Not much has changed and it's a 'good read' either way – and a great way to get a sense of what went on.

ACTIVITY 4.1: Feminist history where you are?

This is an optional activity for anyone studying outside of the US and UK. Now would be a good time to explore what you can of the history of feminism in social psychology in your country. In many places there will be an organisation (such as the New Zealand Psychologists Board, the Icelandic Psychological Association, or the Singapore Psychological Society) that should give you a good start. But also look for other sources, as women's history is often somewhat hidden.

SECTION SUMMARY

- Social psychology has a long history of misogyny and of excluding women, and a long legacy of women who have fought against it. Much of the early feminist scholarship has been lost, as it rarely got published, and then only in very obscure places.
- We are indebted to the women who brought about the changes that have enabled us to engage in feminist social psychology so successfully. There are still hills to climb, and this Companion is an element in continuing the fight.

Excluding women

Historically, excluding women from elite opportunities reflects the mores of the time, when middle-class women were seen to be delicate, innocent, and modest – in need of being protected from the rough, rowdy, and lecherous behaviour of male students (and staff!). College heads were particularly worried about the impossibility of policing hundreds of young men and women 'of marriageable age' (euphemism for sexually active). Moreover, having women in a class was seen as 'horribly distracting' to the male students (and, more clandestinely, their teachers).

Exclusionary strategies

It is fascinating in a horrifying sort of way to explore the mechanisms that were used by the men in charge to make female scholarship difficult. The following list is based on first-hand accounts by the women who sought to gain qualifications (especially PhDs) in psychology (mostly taken from feministvoices.com and Crawford and Unger, 1997, 2000).

Women were (and are still) excluded by:

- Educational disadvantage, where qualifications are discriminatory, for example in terms of the language used and the ways in which gender and social class are stereotyped. Action towards equity is being taken but this problem still persists.

- Not being given access to places, resources, and the training to develop appropriate skills to make progress, such as advanced ICT training.
- Being paid less and given discriminatory employment contracts.
- Being directed away from high prestige jobs and offered menial jobs only in a take-it-or-leave-it manner.
- Being subtly treated as the '***mules and donkeys***' who do all the menial work.
- Being expected to do the pastoral work – time-consuming emotional labour.
- Being 'left out of the loop' – not being informed about or invited to important formal meetings or social events.
- Not getting given the informal mentoring operating within the 'bro' fraternity. A reluctance to give feedback or support to anyone 'not in the club'.
- Being sexually harassed during your job interview, or belittled in other ways.
- Behaviour at conferences, conventions, and other public events that demeans and humiliates women and Others – such as lectures being ended by a picture of a bikini-clad (or even nude) woman. This is presented as a 'joke' – and 'not finding it funny' then used as evidence that women do not have a sense of humour.
- Women being judged by their looks and form of dress rather than their academic competence. Praise is given for 'looking gorgeous today' rather than for 'writing an elegant and informative' paper.
- Not seen as having 'leadership potential' and therefore not selected for leadership training.

ACTIVITY 4.2: Reflecting on exclusionary practice

Go through the list and identify those strategies to which you have been subjected. Add any other forms of hostility and unfairness you have experienced Then reflect on how it made you feel, and the practical consequences for you. This activity is mainly about 'consciousness-raising' – getting a real sense of what is at stake. But the activity works better if you can do it in a group.

If you are a woman or other discriminated-against person: consider how you can get together with others to work out what you can do collectively about it.

If you are a straight, White, privileged male: make notes on each of the points in the list and draft strategies whereby you can be one of the 'good guys' – men committed to creating a more socially just work environment, who actively strive not to abuse the powers accorded to them because of their gender. How can you be an effective ally to women and others who face disadvantage? Again, consider working together with others.

SECTION SUMMARY

- Early feminist social psychologists were subjected to a barrage of exclusionary action. While in some places much of this has now become illegal, we live in a world where there is little attempt to regulate it or require compliance, and it still goes on.
- If we want things to change, we need to take action ourselves. Identifying what is wrong with what is happening now is a good way to start.

Male violence against women

Fin Mackay, a powerful activist and academic who organised *Reclaim the Night* protests in the 1970s (and has been reviving them more recently), regards male sexual violence towards women as *the* most important harm that patriarchy promotes and condones. For her, feminists must not just strive for equity and inclusion, but are obliged to tackle the sheer volume of male violence towards women. She defines it as including 'rape, domestic abuse, forced marriage, sexual assault, child sexual abuse, stalking, sexual exploitation in prostitution and trafficking for prostitution, female genital mutilation and so-called "honour crimes"' (Mackay, 2015, p. 9). We would add the violence of making abortion illegal, as the impact of unsafe 'backstreet abortions' can cause severe damage to women and can be fatal. This list brings together a wide range of actions, reminding us that male violence towards women is a complex matter, with a range of different justifications for what is being done.

> **See and hear for yourself**
> Fin Mackay is a brilliant speaker and it is well worth listening to her radical take on feminism. Find the link to her TED talk on 'What is feminism?' on YouTube. If possible, watch it together with somebody else – or, better still, with a group of others, so you can discuss what she is saying.

Male and female crime

Estimating crime rates is notoriously difficult but in terms of gender one thing stands out: crime is a masculine phenomenon. In 2017, the best estimate of gender difference among known criminals in England and Wales was that around 83% of them were men and boys, and for those convicted or cautioned for sexual assaults, 98% men and boys. As well as being less likely to engage in crime and to commit crimes that are less serious, unlike boys girls tend not to be drawn into a life of crime. Indeed, the only crime that is recognised as predominantly *female* is prostitution – which perhaps says more about the law that patriarchy has created than about female criminality. Women's motivations also tend to be different – less about 'thrill seeking' and being part of a gang, and more about getting money to feed their kids.

We argue that gender differences in crime – and especially violent crime – should not be attributed to male biology. As human beings, men are capable of being thoughtful and self-aware, meaning that they can, through rational thought and empathy, reflect upon their beliefs and behaviours and change them – or simply eschew violence all together. It is insulting, surely, to view men as inherently testosterone-fuelled, violent, and sexually predatory beings, incapable of resisting their biological urges? This treats men as if they were no more than their biology and refuses to acknowledge their fundamental human-ity and capacity for being decent and considerate.

Domestic abuse and its roots in patriarchy

Having said that, the data on male violence towards women, especially within the family home, is truly shocking. It is salutary to recognise that while men are at their safest when at home, for women it is where they are at most at risk. We do need to take it seriously and invest in finding ways to make it 'unthinkable' for men to attack women in their homes – and thus make it a lot less 'doable'. Yet there is a long way to go! According to a survey commissioned by Australia's National Research Organisation for Women and Safety (**ANROWS**) in 2016, almost one in seven young Australians state that a man would be entitled to rape a woman if she had encouraged him to get intimate but then changed her mind (Davey, 2019). This is a thought-provoking example of just how persistent patriarchy's influence has been, and just how dangerous it is. And, especially, how important it is for people to realise that it is not evolution, savage in tooth and claw, that makes us human, but socialisation and enculturation.

ACTIVITY 4.3: Violence in people's homes

It is an important part of feminism to inform yourself about violence in the family home. Conduct an Internet search to find a good definition of 'domestic abuse' (the UK *Refuge* website gives a very detailed one; so too does the UK Government). Notice that 'abuse' does not mean just physical violence but includes actions such as emotional abuse and coercive control. Then search to find out about the rate of domestic (or 'intimate') vio-lence happening in the country or district where you live. Look at a range of situations and make sure you take the degree of violence into account, and the rate of repeat incidents, as this tends to differ between male and female offenders. If you cannot find local statistics, do go elsewhere, as locally as you can – it matters that you get a sense of just how pervasive this problem is. Once you have the statistics, reflect upon them, and, if you can, make some notes on what you think about:

- the impact of this amount of violence in the family home on the victims;
- the impact on any children living in the home;
- the impact on women in general;
- the impact on men in general.

Sexual harassment

It may surprise you to know that the term 'sexual harassment' is relatively new. Enloe writes poignantly about the way that, in the 1970s, women began to use this term. W.S.R. certainly remembers feeling so much better when we had a term that we could use to call out male behaviour we had found distressing. Before, we just didn't have the language to talk about it – let alone question it! We were just expected to 'laugh it off' as 'boys being boys'; put up with it and not tell anyone for fear we would be seen as having brought it on ourselves. At that time, a fair proportion of men believed that such behaviours were a genuine entitlement – it was perfectly okay (just a little bit naughty – oh what fun!) to furtively fondle the bodies of young girls or lure your students into your office and force awkward kisses on them – or worse, expose yourself with a prurient smirk and an invitation. (This actually did happen to somebody W.S.R. knows.)

Fifty years later, sexual harassment is generally acknowledged as unacceptable, and in some cases positively criminal, as movie mogul Harvey Weinstein has found to his cost. The old excuses are recognised as disingenuous and the **#MeToo movement** has encouraged women to speak out about incidents in their past. Gradually, it is becoming recognised that sexual harassment and rape have more to do with the misuse of power over the vulnerable than anything to do with men's 'uncontrollable sexual urges' or 'youthful indiscretions'. An excellent resource here is Lisa Lazard's book, *Sexual Harassment, Psychology and Feminism: #MeToo, Victim Politics and Predators in Neoliberal Times* (2020). It offers a comprehensive coverage of the #MeToo movement, and harassment of men as well as women.

So, what's social psychology got to do with it?

Rather a lot, actually! In a ground-breaking paper by Jacy Young and Peter Hegarty (2019), we discover some pretty horrid stuff. In what they call social psychology's *'masculinist scientific culture'*, they document its manifestations and its consequences. These fall into two key categories: experiments that used sexual harassment as a means to do research; followed by an account of how the masculinist culture created the conditions in which sexual harassment could flourish.

Sexual harassment used for experimental manipulation

In the 1950s and 1960s, social psychology became rather obsessed with the topic of cognitive dissonance – the uncomfortable and unsettling feelings aroused by simultaneously holding incompatible beliefs or attitudes. Early research in this field was led by Leon Festinger and his loyal team of male students. At the time when experimental social psychology was being established, there were no ethics committees to regulate how experiments were run. So, when this state was induced experimentally, it was often done in deceitful and deceptive ways. In this research, the hypothesis being tested was that a severe initiation increased people's loyalty to the group and made them value it more. That is, the more unpleasant the event that leads to gaining entry to an elite group, the more valuable group membership was seen to be. Two young men – Elliot Aronson and Judson Mills, working as part of Festinger's team – conducted and published what has become a nastily notorious experiment, 'The effect of severity of initiation on liking for a group'. In the experiment, these two men induced cognitive dissonance by having female subjects read out to one of them, Aronson, '12 obscene words, e.g., fuck, cock, and screw' as well as 'vivid descriptions of sexuality from contemporary novels' (Aronson & Mills, 1959, p. 178). The women in the control group were required to call out only inoffensive words and texts.

The words and text were deliberately chosen to be as disturbing and distressing as possible – sufficiently embarrassing and humiliating to generate the experimental effect required. Today, their 'severe initiation' feels more like *actual* sexual harassment. Mills later boasted that the reason the experiment yielded such clear data was because it was so cleverly designed. Nobody seems to have questioned the legitimacy of these two male experimenters deliberately distressing a group of young women in order to make an experiment work, until Ian Lubek and Hank Stam put their heads above the parapet (Lubek & Stam, 1995).

SECTION SUMMARY

- Criminality is a slippery thing to measure – it depends how you define it and how you get your data (as seen in 2020 around the BLM protests in the USA). Nevertheless, it does appear to be a highly gendered phenomenon, with more than 90% of sexual violence committed by men against women and children.
- We dispute that this is simply the consequence of male biology – that men have evolved to have 'violent urges' and 'irresistible sexual needs'.
- Sexual harassment must also be taken seriously, not just because it is wrong but because it uses the fear it engenders to control and contain women. Its 'acceptance' within a masculinist culture can and does cause serious damage to many women's careers, not to mention their wellbeing.

Sexual harassment encouraged by the workings of masculinist culture

By the late 1970s, concerns about sexual harassment within psychology led to a survey in the USA, the results of which were published in *Scientific American* (Pope, Levenson, & Schover, 1979). And the results were truly shocking. The survey provided a body of evidence about the impact of sexual harassment on women in psychology. Young and Hegarty (2019) draw extensively on this evidence to make their case. They powerfully convey the feelings of helplessness, disillusionment, and self-blame experienced by a young woman in the 1970s arriving at work to find sexually explicit notes passed under the door of her office, sent by 'a colleague in a position to judge my work'. Another woman academic talks of how senior colleagues warned her to 'stop rocking the boat … just do your job and shut up, be good girls'.

The issue came to a head in social psychology around the notorious and persistent sexual predation of Henri Tajfel, who is famous and revered for developing the concept of social identity and often regarded as the founding father of modern social psychology. The European Association for Social Psychology set up a lifetime achievement prize in his name. In 2019, however, the EASP removed his name from the award. This decision initiated a controversy among social psychologists that is still raging.

Tajfel was appointed to a chair in social psychology at Bristol in 1967. Young and Hegarty (2019) give a detailed account of the way in which his behaviour was very much a reflection of the masculinist (or simply patriarchal) academic climate within which he operated at Bristol. It is a set-up that was typical for many university psychology departments in the 1960s and 1970s, where academic alpha-males headed up teams or 'labs' of graduate students and researchers, bringing in external funding and kudos for the university. They thought they could get away with anything.

Making changes

This last section consists of a single activity, to get you better informed and develop the skills and gain the knowledge you will need to build a feminist future (and yes, men can be feminists too). It is, of course, optional. But developing your own database should help you to improve your future life-experiences, reduce your own risks, and enable you to support others.

ACTIVITY 4.4: Legal and Institutional remedies

First, do an Internet search around the laws where you live about:

- equal opportunities law, especially in relation to employment, including recruitment procedures, maternity leave, health and safety;
- criminal law with respect to domestic abuse, sexual harassment, sexual assault, and stalking;
- abortion law.

Make some notes and, if you have time, try to find out how the laws differ in other countries. Next, download the Codes of Conduct and arrangements for making a complaint where you study or work. Find out how complaints procedures actually operate. Next, explore the support services available to you – generically (such as a national rape crisis line), locally (in your nearest town), and specifically where you work. Make a record of phone numbers, email addresses, and websites – including those for the local police.

Finally, explore your community or friendship group. Maybe even get together to organise some activism that will help to make changes.

CHAPTER SUMMARY

- Historically, patriarchy was the dominant worldview, limiting the life-opportunities of women and rendering them vulnerable to exploitation and violence. In some parts of the world, this worldview is gradually being eroded, opening up opportunities for women and changing prevailing attitudes and beliefs about what is right and just in terms of gender.

- Women pioneers fought this prejudice, and gradually gained a foothold and developed careers in social psychology. Today, there is still no level playing field, and the fight needs to continue.

- Social psychology has a 'horrible history' in its attitudes to and beliefs about women. Not only did this result in massive inequity, it also failed to recognise the impact of sexual harassment. Even as late as the 1960s, experiments were being run that used sexual harassment of young women as an *experimental variable.* In addition, a masculinist culture often operated within social psychology departments, where people 'turned a blind eye' to sexual misconduct.

- The law and employment systems have changed significantly in relation to tackling inequality and sexual violence. Women and others who are vulnerable to the misuse of power now have recourse to enable them to challenge behaviour that is wrong.

5 Prejudice, stereotyping, and objectification

Learning objectives

Study of this chapter (including its activities) should enable you to:
- Have a better awareness and appreciation of how both explicit and implicit gender bias shapes behaviour and norms.
- Confront your own biases and reflect upon where they come from, how they are maintained, and what you can do to resist them.
- Learn about how social psychology is shifting from an interest in a kind of prejudice that is firmly located in the individual to a more holistic view of Othering, which considers the systemic, cultural, and more insidious ways that different groups (mis)treat each other.
- Become more aware of how prejudice of different groups can be understood through a feminist lens.
- Better understand the different ways that women are stereotyped and discriminated against, such as the objectification of women and the 'brain/body divide' misrepresenting women, and how it can be challenged and tackled.

Gendered biases and assumptions

To get us thinking about how gender biases guide daily life, we have a riddle for you!

A man is driving along a road with his son. Suddenly, their car crashes and the man and son are rushed to different hospitals. When the young boy is taken into theatre, the surgeon exclaims: 'I can't possibly perform this surgery – this is my son!'. How is this possible?

Did you get it? The answer, of course, is that the surgeon is the boy's mother. However, the notion of a woman surgeon goes so far against our implicit gender bias, that this riddle still genuinely stumps people. When M.P. saw this circulate on Facebook, the comment section was an entertaining read. 'Did the father get a taxi to the son's hospital?', one commenter offered. Or, more commonly, perplexed commenters queried, 'Was the surgeon the boy's biological father, and the other man ... wasn't?'. The pages of responses grapple endlessly with the notion that there is a fundamental mismatch between some social representations in our heads (in this case, being a surgeon) and being a woman.

These reactions demonstrate how pervasive gender bias can be. Before being prompted to consider their assumptions, people initially find it inconceivable that a woman can be a surgeon. And we can't really blame them – after all, this kind of gendered messaging about what men and women are (or, indeed, what they *should* be) is transmitted to us from the moment we are given our first dolly to coo over. Indeed, feminist social psychology research demonstrates that from an early age, children are exposed to gender stereotypic information about what men and women are, could be, and should be (Martin, 2005). Because of this insidious messaging, children readily endorse these gender stereotypes from as young as three years of age (Martin & Ruble, 2004) and can make accurate categorisations based on gender in preschool. Gender stereotypes are transmitted to children in various explicit and implicit ways, including the gendering of clothes and toys – all sorts of gender stereotypes abound in media marketing.

Systematic subordination

It is important to note that prejudice, stereotyping, and ***Othering*** of women results from ***'systemic subordination*** rather than as the result of individual, accidental, or coincidental misfortune' (Mann, 2012, p. 9). That is, interpersonal theories of prejudice often position prejudice as something that occurs on a targeted, localised level, rather than being the product of something altogether larger and more systemic. This prejudice derives broadly from schemas – referred to by DiMaggio (1997) as a pattern of behaviour which acts as a framework and representation of our ***worldview***. Bem (1981) identified that for those individuals whose sex is explicitly assigned (the 'sex-typed'), all social information is processed through the lens of their gendered schemas.

Despite evidence of some rare instances of the equal distribution of power between men and women, generally speaking 'power tilts towards men' (Wood & Eagly, 2002, p. 712) pretty well universally. This has been used to explain the global crisis of women-directed sexual harassment and rape (Lorber, 2000). It shows how a culture's approach to gender roles shapes the self-concept and behaviours of its members, usually to the detriment of females. As Condor summarises: 'sex roles restrict women's participation in the political and economic world of men' (1986, p. 104).

What is prejudice?

The feminists have destroyed the old image of woman, but they could not erase the hostility, the prejudice, the discrimination that still remained.
– Betty Friedan, *The Feminine Mystique* (1963)

To start to understand how prejudice is defined and understood, first imagine that you are the captain of a netball team in high school. You are faced with a group of players and you must select, one by one, your hopefully winning team. Who do you pick? How do you make this decision? Do you carefully and analytically weigh up the perceived pros and cons of each player, or do you 'go with your gut'? Are there groups of people who you automatically go to, and groups that you automatically disregard? And is this *prejudice?*

The implications of your decision in this context aren't hugely important in the grand scheme of things. But now, consider that instead of selecting your school netball team, you're instead selecting the next psychology graduate intern at your business from a list of potential applicants. Or you're selecting who to befriend at a university party. Or who to vote for in a US presidential election. We make social judgements on a daily basis all the time. We decide who we want to befriend, who to cross the street for, and who to trust. Therefore, given the vast array of social information and decision-making with which we are bombarded, we need shortcuts. Social psychologists call these heuristics or schemas, which are ultimately person-perception short-cuts. We rely on bits of information that we have, coupled with our 'gut instinct' about people, to decide whether they are friend or foe. Problematically, however, feminist social psychologists have demonstrated how misguided these judgements can be and how scant the information we often have upon which to make important decisions about other people.

Prejudice is, essentially, a negative or hostile attitude towards members of particular groups, simply as a result of their group membership. In the 1950s in the UK, for example, it was common to see notices outside lodging houses stating: 'NO IRISH'. These days prejudice is often more insidious and hidden – like banning certain Irish names from the guests you will accept at your holiday camp. It is where our thinking leads us directly into the ways in which biases of this kind create the conditions for prejudice. Behaving in prejudicial ways is often unintended, but powerfully written into our gut reactions, our well-established and over-learned memories, and our perceptions. Prejudice research is perhaps one of the most lively and dynamic bodies of research in the mainstream social psychology literature just now.

Although their language is situated firmly within mainstream **epistemologies**, Ferguson, Branscombe, and Reynolds (2019), for example, provide an interesting account of how social change and prejudice research can inform and advance each other. They have explored the process of how social change in society, and reappraisals of old methodologies in social psychology, can enable new aspects of prejudice to be examined. They propose that 'as researchers use their scientific tools differently, they discover and embrace new sources of evidence – ones that were previously overlooked or misinterpreted. Consequently, prejudice research comes to represent a type of collective, scientific action mobilized in support of group interested social change' (2019, p. 2).

Implicit versus explicit prejudice

Importantly, social psychological research demonstrates that (funnily enough!) the vast majority of people don't see themselves as biased or prejudiced.

Generally, we don't like to think of ourselves as people capable of acting in a prejudiced or biased way. To understand this a little more, the difference between explicit prejudice (i.e. that which is overt, intentional, and conscious) and implicit prejudice (i.e. the conditioned, unconscious, covert biases) provides some useful context. Some social psychologists have suggested that implicit biases guide behaviour. In a nice example of a feminist social psychological study that uses experimental methodologies, Bailey, LaFrance, and Dovidio (2020) demonstrate how people generally associate 'humanity' or human qualities more readily with men that with women. The authors suggest that this demonstrates a 'men are human, women are gendered' effect, which sees men as 'default human' and women as a gendered 'version' of this default.

This notion that prejudice need not be overt or explicit (a) to exist or (b) be harmful is echoed throughout feminist social psychological scholarship. Much like the research into bystander apathy, in which people are wary to intervene in a crisis, prejudice research also demonstrates that people generally think of themselves as good, moral people who are on the 'right side' of prejudice. For example, research shows that bystander apathy regularly occurs in *sexist* communication, in that sexist remarks are neither confronted by the victims of the comments nor nearby bystanders (Becker, Zawadzki, & Shields, 2014). As an extension of this, Koudenburg et al. (2020) demonstrated that conversation flow affects perceptions of sexist communication, and very subtle variations in how people respond to a sexist statement in a group setting can have a strong influence on how bystanders make judgements about the sexist content.

ACTIVITY 5.1: Confronting our implicit associations

Visit the website https://implicit.harvard.edu/implicit/ or google 'Project Implicit' and take a look at their range of Implicit Association Tests (IATs): they are delivered online where the test-taker is asked to make rapid judgements about different groupings of people. Supposedly, the rapidness of IATs means that they are able to 'bring to light' our otherwise hidden, implicit biases. For example, someone who has an *implicit* racist bias will be slower (we are talking milliseconds) to associate a photo of a Black woman with the word 'good' than a photo of a White woman. When you enter the website, you will see that there is a wide range of tests which are designed to show implicit biases towards a number of different groups, including women, Black people, transgender people, older people, and many more. Select one of these IATs to do yourself. You can choose any of them – they are all designed to show implicit biases and the various forms that they can take.

Consider the following questions:

- How did you find the process of taking the 'test'?
- Did it feel (un)comfortable? Were you at ease?
- Do you think that there are elements of either being prejudiced and experiencing prejudice that this kind of online test isn't able to capture?
- Is this a useful tool?
- Is this a feminist tool?

While the robustness of IATs has been questioned recently in the context of social psychology's 'Replication Crisis' (we'll get to this in Chapter 6), the IAT is a good proxy for implicit biases. Some social psychologists have reported that the process of doing an IAT can actually engender attitude and behaviour change. It can, therefore, be a powerful teaching tool. Adams et al. (2014), for example, suggest that if students are made aware of their implicit associations, via this test, then it can raise their awareness of prejudice, stereotyping, and discrimination.

SECTION SUMMARY

- So far in this chapter, we have considered the definition of prejudice from a feminist perspective, including noting the difference between implicit and explicit biases.
- We have used the IAT to uncover the tricky business of realising, and subsequently confronting, gender biases.
- Gender stereotypes, norms, and expectations can consolidate and hence lead to *systemic subordination* of groups, such as women, in which groups are marginalised or silenced.

Othering

Feminist social psychologists have also noted that individual prejudice can lead to the chronic, systemic, and collective Othering of groups of people. As an extension of prejudice, the notion of 'Othering' is tangled up in the idea of speaking 'for' or 'about' other groups. The term arguably originates from Simone de Beauvoir's (1949) classic text *The Second Sex*, in which she writes that women, broadly, 'are defined and differentiated with reference to man and not he with reference to her ... He is the Subject, he is the Absolute – she is the Other' (1949/1997, p. 16). Those who are 'Othered' are essentially constructed as inferior or abnormal; as Kitzinger and Wilkinson (1996) put it, women are socially positioned to be 'objects of male knowledge', which serves to silence and oppress women. 'Othering' is concerned with the tricky tension of representation and power and prompts us to question the value of speaking 'on behalf' of Othered groups.

It is important that notions of Othering do not rely solely on the assumption that gender unites all women 'more powerfully than race and class divides them' (Gluck & Patai, 1992, p. 2). Black feminist psychologists have stressed how women experience oppression in unique ways; women of colour's experiences of Othering are distinct from those of White women, as it is tangled up with racism, White supremacy, and colonialism (Kitzinger & Wilkinson, 1996). Therefore, as with any feminist discussion, we should be conscious of how conversations about Othering have been predominately voiced by White women, which may reinforce the *discourse* of Other (see Mohanty, 1988). Therefore, an intersectional approach to Othering, as ever, is important. See Chapter 4 for a more comprehensive discussion on the value of intersectionality and acknowledging how race, social class, and (dis)ability intersect with gender.

Feminist psychology as 'Other'

Beyond feminist social psychology conversations about Othering, some scholars have noted how feminist psychology *itself* is marginalised and positioned as inferior. As Eagly and Riger (2014) argue, feminist scholars who critique the postpositivist epistemology that dominates psychology operate very much on 'the margins of the discipline'. It may indeed be argued that feminist psychology itself has historically been marginalised or 'Othered' from mainstream discourses of psychology (MacArthur & Shields, 2014; Rutherford, Vaughn-Blount, & Ball, 2010).

SECTION SUMMARY

- We have moved on from the more mainstream notion of prejudice and have also noted how 'Othering' goes hand in hand with a feminist appraisal of prejudice.
- Othering is a much more systemic, powerful phenomenon than prejudice, where certain groups are not only made the object of personal prejudice, but also are systematically marginalised in mainstream spaces. Their experiences become side-lined, seen as not to matter and viewed as 'alien'.

(Sexual) objectification of women

I (M.P.) vividly remember being in the first year of my psychology degree and developing a love for performance poetry (otherwise known by the glorious title '*slam poetry*'). I spent hours on YouTube watching brilliant, articulate poets take to the microphone and air their frustrations, thoughts, feelings, and ideas in the form of the powerful spoken word. Among my favourites is a slam poem by the American feminist poet Brenda Twohy, which discusses the sexual dissection and *objectification* of women in mass media. My favourite line is this: '*Don't you give me raw meat and tell me it is nourishment, I know a slaughterhouse when I see one*'. In the poem, Twohy shows how women's bodies are routinely cut up into 'small, marketable pieces', so much so that 'you can almost forget they were ever real bodies'. It's a triumph of a poem and introduces the topic of sexual objectification exquisitely.

Indeed, beyond the concept of Othering, feminist social psychologists have also pointed out how groups of people, including women, are objectified so thoroughly that they become (quite literally) dehumanised. Prejudice occurs at many different levels and to a wide range of different groups. Some feminist scholars have noted that extreme forms of prejudice can lead to the dehumanisation of people, which can have its own set of uniquely negative consequences. *Infrahumanisation*, for example, is an extreme instantiation of prejudice, which sees one group being perceived as less than 'human' on account of their group membership. Infrahumanisation is a form of dehumanisation; some groups are so hideously prejudiced against that they are (quite literally) denied their humanity.

See and hear for yourself

I (M.P.) have learnt a lot about feminism through slam poetry (or 'performance poetry'). My favourite 'hub' of slam poetry is the organisation Button Poetry, which has its own YouTube channel. Interested? Then have a listen to the poems of Blythe Baird, Brenda Twohy, or Sarah Kay there. They are all fabulous feminists who speak to a lot of the content of this Companion!

Objectification theory

I don't feel like a woman unless I look like a chandelier.

– Swati Sharma (2018)

Extending the notion of dehumanisation, *objectification theory* (Fredrickson & Roberts, 1997) argues that women are consistently objectified and dehumanised by society. Objectification is the process of reducing a woman to a 'sum of her parts', rather than viewing her as a full, complete, living, breathing human being. Objectification theorists argue that there is an omnipresent critical scrutiny of the female body, which prompts women to be perceived as quite *literally* (Heflick & Goldenberg, 2014) more object-like and less human than men.

Aapola, Gonick, and Harris offer a neat summary of objectification, explaining how 'young women are encouraged to relate to their bodies as objects that exist for the use and aesthetic pleasure of others' (2005, p. 136). This, as you might expect, can lead to a whole host of negative outcomes, such as habitual body monitoring, higher body shame, appearance anxiety, and depression. Sexual objectification of women occurs regularly in the media, popular culture, and online. As a testament to this, research shows that the average female university student notices herself or other women being sexually objectified about twice a day (Holland et al., 2017). In Rachel Calogero's gloriously titled paper 'Objects don't object!' (2013), she shows that objectification not only harms cognitive performance and makes women feel bad and 'less than'; crucially, feeling like that stops women protesting – and that's how they get away with it! The more women are dehumanised and objectified, the less agency women feel they have to resist, disrupt, and protest. And so the cycle rolls on and on.

This whole objectification/***empowerment*** debacle ultimately derives from the fundamental notion that people perceive women's *brains* and *bodies* as inherently at odds with each other (Heflick et al., 2011). This is in line with the notion that what we see and how we see it is often constructed by and for 'the ***male gaze***'. In terms of gender and sexuality, this perspective is the product of how predominantly male film directors and financiers provide men with 'visual pleasure'. They do it by turning women into objects out on display for men's sensuous gratification. Note that this is a communal enterprise, happening so relentlessly that movie-goers don't notice.

Importantly – and unfortunately – it is all too easy for women to internalise these perceptions so that they become ***self-objectified***, leading to all manner of negative consequences. Specifically, when self-objectification gets drawn into women's awareness of their sense of their own embodiment – women come to view themselves differently. In a classic demonstration of this effect, Barbara Fredrickson and Tomi-Ann Roberts (1997) and Fredrickson *et al.* (1998) showed how self-objectification can have consequences in different contexts. In their experimental study, women completed a difficult maths test whilst wearing either a swimsuit, which was designed to elicit feelings of self-objectification, or a baggy, comfortable jumper, which did not. When women completed the task alone whilst wearing a swimsuit, they performed badly on the maths task. When they repeated the experiment in the jumper with men, there was no reduction in their competence. The finding that self-objectification harms cognitive performance has been replicated in multiple different conditions and settings (see, for example, Winn & Cornelius, 2020).

'Girl Power' and challenging sexism

Social psychology seeks to understand how people collude in, amplify, and reinforce prejudice and Othering. Learning how social psychology can explain the resistance of prejudice and bias is also an important achievement. This is particularly true for interpersonal prejudice, as opposed to the systemic, institutional kind of prejudice that occurs on a daily basis. As Hyers (2007) eloquently explains, *interpersonal prejudice* or sexism may provide a forum for women to 'engage in activism'. However, this lure for activism and self-advocacy often conflicts with the socially imposed diktat that women must be 'passive and accommodating'. In other words, interpersonal sexism is a useful space to challenge sexism one-to-one, but this is often difficult given the mandate to 'be nice' that women must contend with. For example, the stereotypical assumption that women will be 'relationship smoothers' (Henley & Freeman, 1989) who rally around to iron out interpersonal tensions is in direct conflict with women wanting to challenge sexism. When this is coupled with the cultural mandate not to be aggressive, confrontational, or difficult, this makes it very hard for women to complain when exposed to sexist taunts.

However, despite these pesky societal pressures, we know that the act of confronting and resisting negative gender stereotypes can be empowering, important, and self-protective (e.g. Mallet & Wagner, 2011). Social psychology research shows how a sense of empowerment and a feeling of having your own 'voice' can make it so much easier for women to reject stereotypes more confidently and more vocally. Empowerment leads to increased self-worth, which in turn enables individuals to collectively bring about social change. In recent years, many mainstream companies have adopted the #feminist 'empowerment' rhetoric to sell their products. 'Be your own kind of beautiful!' they tell us, 'find your voice, girls!', 'stand up to The Man!'.

Some feminist scholars have raised concerns about this kind of 'empowerment marketing'. For instance, Emilie Zaslow does so in her book *Feminism Inc.: Coming of Age in Girl Power Media Culture* (2009). There she examines the interplay between popular media and the empowerment/objectification message, and stresses that promoting these girl-power empowerment-based marketing messages 'does not require an investment in social change'. It can be tokenistic and trivialising if not accompanied by action. As Driscoll also cautioned: 'can merchandised relations to girls be *authentic*?' (1999, p. 178). This has also leaked its way into popular culture, including music, which we'll explore together in the next activity.

ACTIVITY 5.2: Objectification or empowerment?

Now, locate the UK Top 40 Chart at the time that you are reading this book. You can easily find this on any radio website. Select a song, sung by a woman, that is at the top of the current charts and watch its official music video on YouTube, whatever it may be. Assess it critically, with your budding critical feminist eye. You may want to look at several if you have time – to get a sense of what is going on.

Ask yourself the following questions:

- Are the women in the videos *empowered*? What does 'empowerment' look like?
- Are the women in these videos being *objectified*? Are they self-objectifying? Have they internalised a 'male gaze'?
- Can the answer to both of these questions be 'yes'?

The question of whether or not a depiction of women 'counts' as 'being feminist' is a tricky thing to grapple with. Feminist scholars, including sociologists, psychologists, and media experts, have discussed this at great length. Take 'The Spice Girls', for example. Some have argued that the hyper-femininity of The Spice Girls serves to commodify feminism by using the discourse of 'Girl Power' to feed the corporate machine that is the music industry ('I'll tell you what I want, what I *really, really* want!'). However, other scholars, including Dafna Lemish (2003), have argued that The Spice Girls offer the opportunity of *multiple feminisms*, such that each Spice Girl demonstrated a varied form of 'legitimate' and 'attainable' feminism. In this way, The Spice Girls took feminism into the mainstream.

In 2020, Cardi B and Megan Thee Stallion made waves with their (now infamously viral) song WAP (or 'Wet Ass Pussy'). In this song, the women vocalists discuss, in some fairly explicit detail, their sexual wants and desires. The response to WAP provided a fascinating window into the heart of society's views on women's sexual liberation. The song faced (quite predictably) a conservative backlash online; one commentator tweeted that '[the song is] *what happens when children are raised without God and without a strong father figure*' – you have to laugh! Similarly, some feminist commentators decried the song as a vulgar, gawdy caricature of feminine sexuality. On the other side of the WAP discourse, young women on social media, including the video platform TikTok, embraced the song as an anthem of Black women 'taking back' their sexuality.

The tension between responses to the WAP saga is emblematic of other objectification/empowerment discourses. For example, Wood (2016) interviewed British women about their experiences of buying and wearing sexy lingerie. Wood noted how the women in the study showed 'complex and often incongruous strategies of accommodation and negotiation' of the lingerie. The act of wearing lingerie was deemed implicitly to be a 'performance of femininity' but one which also allowed women to 'resist some of the respectable norms of female sexuality' (2016, p. 10). This echoes women's responses to WAP and summarises neatly the tricky business of understanding objectification and empowerment. Our question to you, therefore, is this: can these overt displays of feminist sexuality be enjoyable, playful, and pleasurable, even when they are judged to be compliant with the objectification of women?

SECTION SUMMARY

- Objectification theory shows how women's bodies are routinely 'dissected' by society, resulting in the perception of women as (literally) less human and more object-like. This can have drastic consequences for women, including disordered eating and negative self-concept.
- The tension between what 'counts' as objectification and what serves to 'empower' women is messy. We've covered a couple of examples where social psychologists, including feminists, disagree in interpretation.

Gender stereotyping

Women's experiences of gender discrimination and feminist protests concerning a contemporary backlash against women reflect women's inroads into traditionally masculine arenas, especially their efforts to gain access to high-status, high-paying, male-dominated jobs, which are thought to require characteristics stereotypically ascribed to men. (Eagly and Mladinic, 1994, p. 2)

We know by now that gender inequality persists. For example, women frequently experience sexual harassment and institutional gender-based prejudice; they face staunchly governed gender norms that limit women's participation in all kinds of fascinating stuff, and thus are subject to a lack of career advancement opportunities compared with men. Stereotypes about women's abilities contribute to this social inequality. A massively influential example is the enduring stereotype that women are 'naturally' intellectually inferior to men, are less competent and lack agency (Eagly & Wood, 2011). It is crucial that we know as much as we can about gender stereotypes because of how much they govern people's expectations and behaviour (Moss-Racusin et al., 2012). Negative gender stereotypes have seriously harmful consequences for women, including restricting women's access to traditionally masculine fields such as science and engineering (Good, Rattan, & Dweck, 2012), reducing women's leadership aspirations, and distorting their performance evaluations.

The Stereotype Content Model, devised by Susan Fiske and her colleagues (Fiske et al., 2002), broadly identifies the contents of the stereotypes adopted by different social groups. Based on the restricted data set of the **majority world**, the model ultimately proposes that people are generally judged against two fundamental qualities: feminine 'warmth' (i.e. kindness, compassion, niceness) and masculine 'competence' (i.e. intelligence, skills, toughness). Warmth and competence broadly exist in a *fourfold taxonomy*, whereby different groups of people are perceived to be generally either high or low on each.

As a general rule, competence is associated with high status and access to power, whereas warmth is associated with being lower down the social food chain. Surprise! Surprise! – women are generally perceived to be warm and incompetent; men competent but cold. Again, within the caveat of the ethnocentric nature of the samples used, this broad stereotype is a robust finding in the social psychological literature (see the meta-analyses by Feingold, 1994 and Cuddy et al., 2009). Women are regularly perceived to promote qualities of traditional femininity (e.g. to be warm, sociable, and kind) and by some kind of weird logic to be therefore incompetent. Or, as an extension of this, if they are perceived to be capable, then they are also seen as being cold (Ebert, Steffens, & Kroth, 2014). It's as though women can't win – inexorably their lives are made complicated and difficult to navigate.

Yet perceptions of warmth and competence are not necessarily mutually exclusive (Fiske et al., 2007). Fiske and her colleagues have proposed that there are four broad reactions to stereotype content, depending on whether an individual is rated as high or low on either or both dimensions. Groups of mixed valence – that is, those who are high on one dimension and low on another – are often met with ambivalent prejudice or, in the context of gender stereotypes, ambivalent sexism. Therefore, the content of the stereotypes informs the nature of the social perception (Cuddy, Fiske, & Glick, 2007):

- *Admiration*:   high warmth and high competence
- *Contemptuous*:   low warmth and low competence
- *Envious*:   high competence and low warmth
- *Paternalistic*: low competence and high warmth

Importantly, these stereotypes about different groups are not only descriptive and categorical, they are prescriptive also. This means that stereotypes don't just describe how groups are, they *dictate* what groups *should* look like and do (Cialdini & Trost, 1998). For example, the overriding stereotype of women as warm but incapable thus dictates that women *should* behave in a way that is passive and subservient (Williams & Best, 1990). Therefore, perhaps unsurprisingly given what we know about how social roles work, people who do not conform or 'fit' to these prescriptive norms are viewed harshly and get a lot of antagonism directed towards them. For example, women working in male-dominated jobs are seen as unfeminine (Badgett & Folbre, 2003), unlikeable (Rudman & Phelan, 2008), cold (Phelan, Moss-Racusin, & Rudman, 2008), and are viewed less positively than women who conform (Eagly & Mladinic, 1994).

Sexism

Glick and Fiske make a distinction between 'benevolent' and 'hostile' sexism as acting in different ways.

> The evidence of the evaluations of female subtypes is consistent with the notion of benevolent sexism as is used to reward women who embrace conventional gender roles and power relations, whereas hostile sexism punishes women who challenge the status quo. This combination of rewards and punishments may be particularly effective in maintaining gender inequality. (2001, p. 113)

Benevolent sexism

Glick and Fiske are suspicious about the motives that '*benevolent sexism*' may have. It is, they conclude, just as much of a power play as hostile sexism, but uses reward rather than punishment. 'Benevolent' sexism is disarming, they say, and intended to be so. It absolves men from being seen as prejudiced, while still enabling them to lay claim to greater power, authority, and earning capacity. They 'need' these things, of course, to be good 'providers' and 'protectors'. They are willing to sacrifice their own needs and wishes in order to properly care for the women in their lives – their wives, their daughters, even their assistants and secretaries. Overall, benevolent sexist ideology serves to limit or even prevent women's participation in masculine realms (Viki, Abrams, & Hutchison, 2003). It is motivated largely by the idea that women, being weak and incapable, require male assistance and protection to cope with their everyday lives (Barreto & Ellemers, 2005). *Protective paternalism* is at the core of benevolent sexism. Offering help is at the heart of protective paternalism and, albeit, maybe, well-intentioned, undermines the autonomy of women (Nadler & Halabi, 2006). Importantly, benevolent sexism is not as readily recognised as being sexist, but exposure to benevolent sexism results in women doubting their competence and cognitive abilities.

There are three sub-components of benevolent sexism:

1 **Protective paternalism:** this is the belief that women's stereotypically ascribed warmth and care mean that they should be protected and provided for by men.
2 **Complementary gender differentiation:** this is the concept that women and men have contrasting but complementary attributes.
3 **Heterosexual intimacy:** the idea that women and men are co-dependent for reasons such as intimacy and reproduction.

PATERNALISTIC PREJUDICE AND PREGNANCY

A group of motherhood activists called 'Pregnant Then Screwed' are brilliant advocates for maternity rights, ending the '**motherhood penalty**', and fighting gender stigma. Their CEO, Joeli Brearley, addressed the crowd at their national conference wearing a t-shirt that read, 'I had a baby, not a lobotomy!'. This slogan sums up the notion of 'paternalistic prejudice' that most pregnant women and new mothers experience. We'll come across more about these kinds of activism groups in Chapter 9.

The notion that women are stereotyped to be essentially warm and incompetent, thus triggering a 'paternalistic' response, is aligned with the 'women are wonderful' effect. This explains the *protective paternalism* that women experience, particularly in times where these distinctions are most prominent, for example, during pregnancy and motherhood (e.g., Sutton, Douglas, & McClellan, 2011). This is seen through the invasive 'giving of advice' to pregnant women, which Robyn Longhurst, a human geographer from New Zealand, has written about extensively.

Hostile sexism

Hostile sexism essentially does what it says on the sexist tin. Seen through a psychoanalytic lens, it is an intentional and explicit hatred of and/or contempt for women and is derived from the concept of chivalry and female dependency. It is deep-rooted, explicitly hostile towards women, and typically fuelled by the belief that women pose a threat to men and must be kept in their place.

Ambivalent sexism

Ambivalent sexism is a more complicated beast. Ambivalent sexism encompasses both positive and negative attitudes towards women and shows how these can often be 'mutually reinforcing ideologies'. As Glick and Fiske (2011, p. 532) elegantly explain, 'benevolent sexism was the carrot aimed at enticing women to enact traditional roles and hostile sexism was the stick used to

Table 5.1: Three forms of sexism identified by feminist social psychology

Types of sexism	Example	Key reading
Benevolent sexism	'Women are wonderful, fair, delicate creatures who we must protect, cherish, and preserve'	Dardenne, B., Dumont, M., & Bollier, T. (2007). Insidious dangers of benevolent sexism: Consequences for women's performance. *Journal of Personality and Social Psychology*, 93(5), 764–779.
Hostile sexism	'I hate women. All women are bitches'	Glick, P., & Fiske, S.T. (1999). The Ambivalence toward Men Inventory: Differentiating hostile and benevolent beliefs about men. *Psychology of Women Quarterly*, 23(3), 519–536.
Ambivalent sexism	'I can't live with women, but I also can't live without them'	Glick, P., & Fiske, S.T. (2001). Ambivalent sexism. In *Advances in experimental social psychology* (Vol. 33, pp. 115–188). London: Academic Press. Glick, P., & Fiske, S.T. (2011). Ambivalent sexism revisited. *Psychology of Women Quarterly*, 35(3), 530–535.

punish them when they resisted'. Both of these forms of sexism serve, somewhat desperately, to maintain a gender-traditional status quo.

To clarify a complex situation, we summarise the three forms of sexism in Table 5.1.

Role congruity theory

Feminist social psychologists have also shown how gender norms dictate certain gendered social roles. Violation of these social roles can lead to hostility and backlash (e.g. Heilman & Wallen, 2010). Any deviation from rigid gender stereotypes can be costly for women in a way that it is not for men (Yoder & Schleicher, 1996). Alice Eagly's notion of role congruity may shed some light on this. Role congruity theory dictates that female leaders face gendered prejudice due to perceived incongruity between being female and being a leader (Eagly & Diekman, 2005). This theory is built on the premise that incongruences between gender and rigid social norms lead to prejudice due to preference for a person of the 'correctly corresponding' gender to fulfil social roles. Role congruity theory may also shed some light on why working mothers in particular face prejudice (Sabat et al., 2016), because the social role of being a 'mother' is at odds with the 'person specification' for being a devoted employee.

SECTION SUMMARY

- In this section, we have considered the *prescriptive* nature of gender stereotypes: the way that gender stereotypes not only describe what behaviours are typically gendered, they also *dictate* what gendered behaviours *should* be. People who defy their corresponding gender norm typically face backlash and are viewed negatively.

- Due to the existence of gender norms and expectations, there are multiple forms of sexism that exist in contemporary society. Importantly, some sexist ideologies (e.g. benevolent sexism) are created by the 'women are wonderful' effect, which is the view that women are delicate creatures in need of help from men. In contrast, other types of sexism are more explicitly negative, such as hostile sexism, which is often considered to be 'women hating' or blatant misogyny.

- We have covered Alice Eagly's work on the *contents* of gender stereotypes, which shows their complex and often nuanced, context-dependent nature.

See and hear for yourself

You will notice that we have drawn heavily on Professor Alice Eagly's work in this chapter. She has accomplished a lot, teasing out the contents of stereotypes, investigating different types of sexism, and exploring the impact of gender norms on behaviour. To learn more about this influential psychologist, you can access her profile on Psychology's Feminist Voices website (www. feministvoices.com). There you will find some interviews, a full biography, and some selected works. It makes for a very inspiring read!

In this chapter, we have considered some meaty issues, such as gender stereotypes, Othering, and prejudice. As Radtke explains, 'the gendered division of labour in a society is presumed to produce gender stereotypes, which are then internalized by the individual to yield a gendered identity' (2017, p. 361). Feminists have called for a more critical consideration of social role theory, by stressing how gender is a performance, always bounded by its social context and situation. Critical feminist scholarship is particularly interested in how history, culture, and social relationships collude to impact upon women's behaviour and gender norms – and how they can be challenged!

CHAPTER SUMMARY

- In this chapter, we have considered the various ways in which feminist thought can shed light on the mainstream's concepts of prejudice, stereotyping, and bias in unique ways. We have explored gender-based prejudice, gender biases, and objectification.

- Taken together, the various theories and perspectives that we've covered throughout this chapter serve to demonstrate how a feminist view of mainstream social psychology allows for a more nuanced and complex picture of person perception. For example, moving from prejudice into Othering allows a more critical and comprehensive understanding of how gender, race, social class, (dis)ability, and other facets of the human experience intersect to inform person perception.

- Some of the concepts in this chapter, such as gender stereotyping, objectification, and gender bias are meaty concepts that will inform most (if not all!) of our discussions throughout this book. As you go through the rest of this Companion book, consider how stereotypes and social norms are informing the other feminist angles that we introduce you to. Arguably, the existence of social norms governed by stereotypes is at the heart of all feminist social psychology!

6   Delusions of gender

Learning objectives

Study of this chapter (including its activities) should enable you to:

- Appreciate how sex difference research may be biased, or at least nowhere near as objective as it comes across.
- Cast a critical eye over the claims being made for hard-wired differences in the brains of men and women, acknowledging how they may lead to essentialist and deterministic conclusions.
- Learn more about the 'Open Science' revolution in social psychology and begin to think about how feminist psychology can both inform and be informed by these recent shifts.
- Reflect upon how the values of feminist psychology can shape, challenge, and align with Open Science as a new way of 'doing' psychological research.

Neurosexism

Most mothers, on some level, feel torn between the pleasures, responsibilities, and pressures of children and their own need for financial or emotional resources. We know that the female brain responds to this conflict with increased stress, increased anxiety, and reduced brainpower for the mother's work and her children.

– Louann Brizendine, *The Female Brain* (2007)

We can assume that Louann Brizendine wrote this book with the best of intentions. She aimed to show how women's brains are designed (or hard-wired) to fulfil certain feminine duties. She also wanted to provide comfort for women who were struggling with keeping up with the challenges of daily life for womankind. 'Don't worry, women!' the book says, 'you're not stupid, your brains just simply aren't designed for anything too complex!' (We're paraphrasing a bit here, of course.) We're not surprised that feminists didn't take too kindly to these claims.

In particular, Cordelia Fine, a Professor of History and Philosophy of Science at the University of Melbourne, took great issue with most of what Brizendine had to say. Her response (Fine, 2008) was a satirical paper that took these ideas about womanhood to task, with a distinctly critical and feminist line of questioning. Fine wryly inquired, 'will working mothers' brains explode?'. In her paper, Fine casts a critical eye over the claims of 'hard-wired' brain differences, and acknowledges that these neuropsychological ideas do have a certain 'seductive allure' (to use the words of Weisberg et al., 2008). But, she says, this is a chimera. She points out that most non-psychologists 'have neither the background nor the resources to question the many inaccurate and misleading claims made about gender differences in the brain' (Fine, 2008, p. 70). In other words, we are often tricked by the impressive-sounding language of neuroscience and thus lack the capacity to question it. Somewhat later, Hoffman and Bluhm (2016) wrote about how these neuroscience claims may constitute '*neurosexism*' – a particularly pretentious form of academic *sexism* – because they often inform assumptions about gender roles.

ACTIVITY 6.1: Cordelia Fine's introduction to neurosexism

To get us started, locate Cordelia Fine's 2008 paper published in *Neuroethics* and give it a read. It's a short, snappy, Open Access paper that provides some nice background to the rest of this chapter.

Fine, C. (2008). Will working mothers' brains explode? The popular new genre of neurosexism. *Neuroethics*, *1*(1), 69–72.

Fine introduces us here to a new idea – neurosexism. Neurosexism, as many feminist social psychologists have gone on to argue, endorses the view that men and women are functionally and essentially different in their neurological makeup. Perhaps more problematically, however, is the notion that women typically come out of theories like these a lot worse than men. Neurosexism has been used to 'put women in their place', often in insidious and sneaky ways, like with Brizendine's cunning book that served to remind women that we are, essentially, not cut out to compete in a world of men. It's built into our brains, so it must be true! The idea of neurosexism is broadly in line with the concept of '*androcentrism*', which views the male as 'default' and anything other than male as 'Other' (you should be familiar now with the concept of *Othering* as a social mechanism from Chapter 5). Bailey, LaFrance, and Dovidio (2020) recently demonstrated that androcentrism is still dominant in popular wisdom.

Traditional research methods have long been regarded as incompatible with feminist research, and while this view is shifting, contemporary scientific methods still operate in the context of patriarchal values, which enforce dominant cultural power hierarchies (D'Ignazio & Klein, 2020). This 'masculinist culture' pervades neuroscience in particular, which is beset with political, ethical, and cultural considerations. This is reflected in the decades-long neuropsychological quest for so-called 'hard-wired' sex differences in men and women's brains. As Cordelia Fine (2010) argues, these neuroscientific investigations may reinforce and legitimise rigid, often misogynistic, gender norms. Neurosexism ultimately endorses an essentialist and determinist approach to gender. It is problematic, as we see it, for three core reasons:

1 It fails to acknowledge the complexity and nuance of gender as a sociocul-turally mediated construct.

2 It also erroneously views sex and gender as binary, when much recent research suggests that they may exist on a spectrum (D'Ignazio & Klein 2020).

3 Claims from the neurosexist literature largely inform our brain-behaviour inferences. For example, as Gina Rippon (2019) notes, sex difference research has traditionally provided 'evidence' for men's greater intellectual ability. Therefore, reports of supposedly 'hard-wired' differences between men and women are weaponised as a means of justifying an unequal distribution of power and correspondingly gendered social roles. This positions men as superior and women as inferior or 'Other'.

So, why are some people so seemingly obsessed with that which is biological or physical? As Bleier (1978) points out, supposed biological explanations for social phenomena are generally widely accepted, because they instil a sense of order and structure to an otherwise subjective world. Scientists (and mainstream psychologists) generally like stuff that is measurable, orderable, and done at a safe distance; it maintains a comforting sense of structure and doesn't challenge the 'illusion of objectivity' so beloved by mainstream social psychologists that we introduced you to in Chapter 2.

However, wherever there are claims of detached objectivity in psychological research, an army of feminist researchers are usually not too far behind! In this case, feminist social psychologists have made good progress in providing alternative stories to the **Big Bio Brigade (BBB)**! For example, Arianne Shahvisi (2020) takes issue with the notion of there being biologically driven 'nesting behaviours' during human pregnancies around preparing a special, nurturing space for the baby-to-come. Isn't this more of a matter of gendered expectations about housework?, she asks. The implications of more recent engagement with biological essentialism can be seen in the backlash against feminism (Ging, 2019), and the rise of the **manosphere** (loosely connected anti-feminist groups, often based online) that often use evolutionary psychology to inform their core ideology on men and women's 'true nature'. In terms of so-called nesting behaviour, we can add to that the impact of **neoliberalism**, which encourages aggressive marketing of all 'the essentials' required to equip the new mother for her new role. Recognise the impact of 'baby showers' and 'gender reveal parties' and the whole edifice of childbirth becomes visible as a massive marketing opportunity. Makes you realise that, in truth, biology hardly gets a look in, does it?

See and hear for yourself

Cordelia Fine's work provides a wonderfully accessible introduction to some of the issues at play here in the neurosexist literature. This 2016 paper by Ginger A. Hoffman and Robyn Bluhm also makes for an interesting read. In the paper, the authors discuss some heavy topics such as the philosophy of science, feminist philosophy, and ethics, to unpick the concepts of neurosexism and **neurofeminism**.

Hoffman, G.A., & Bluhm, R. (2016). Neurosexism and neurofeminism. *Philosophy Compass, 11*(11), 716–729.

Feminist responses to neurosexism

Feminist psychologists and activists have made considerable progress in challenging this work, including evolutionary explanations of sex differences. For example, Anne Fausto-Sterling has written extensively about the problematic inferences drawn from traditional sex difference research. She calls on psychologists also to consider how sex could possibly work as a biological mechanism that produces gender, stressing instead that it is produced by processes of enculturation and socialisation (Fausto-Sterling, 2008). Other feminists, such as Louise Westmarland (2015), an expert in policing, have argued powerfully that biological essentialists within evolutionary psychology and neuroscience are the intellectual arm of the feminism backlash, and challenging them is imperative if we are to stop men being violent to women. Views like this position women as 'needing to be kept in hand'. Yet challenges to mainstream neurosexism are often met with extreme hostility – what feminists have taken to calling *testeria* – the male equivalent of hysteria. Getting emotional like this is not at all surprising, given the historic silencing of disruptive, critical, feminist voices (Rutherford, Vaughn-Blount, & Ball, 2010), particularly in spaces dominated by masculine conventions (like police and military establishments). In order to understand the core concerns that feminists have about the neurosexist literature, there are three important concepts to get your head around. These are: *essentialism, determinism,* and *social constructionism,* which we'll go into briefly here. Some related concepts can also be found in our glossary.

Essentialism: As Janis Bohan argues, saying that something is essentialist 'is not the same as saying that it argues for the biological determinism of gender' (1993, p. 6). Instead, essentialism, in the context of sex differences, dictates that gender is a set of internal and persistent 'fundamental attributes'.

Determinism: Sigrid Schmitz (2010) provides a useful overview of the difference between determinism and constructionism. In essence, biological determinism suggests that one's biology (in this case, one's neurological makeup or brain structure) can directly *determine* certain outcomes. Also, determinists view this biology as pre-determined and fixed, unchangeable by external or social forces.

Constructionism: Constructionism, by contrast, argues that gender is constructed through social judgements about what matters, and what it means. In this sense, gender is a 'performance' of roles and behaviours that are ascribed social meaning by the context within which it operates.

We'll talk about social constructionism a lot more in our discussion about the constructs of language in Chapter 7.

ACTIVITY 6.2: Tracing the feminist debate in the literature

In 1994, the brilliant feminist journal *Feminism & Psychology* featured a lively and important special issue, edited by Celia Kitzinger, entitled 'Should Psychologists Study Sex Differences?'. In the special issue, Kitzinger invited a host of eminent feminist psychologists (our dream party guestlist!) to debate the issue. We invite you now to locate this special issue online – Volume 4, Issue 4, November 1994 – and browse the responses there.

As you are reading the various feminist responses to this question of sex differences, consider the following prompts:

- Is each feminist psychologist arguing for something distinct, or are there a set of shared concerns?
- Who provides the most convincing response, in your opinion?
- Did anything about these responses shock you? Were they in line with your expectations?

Hopefully, after spending some time digesting the arguments of the various feminist 'wise women' in this special issue of *Feminism & Psychology*, you will notice that there is a lot of nuance in these discussions. And as with all psychologists, feminist psychologists don't always agree with each other!

SECTION SUMMARY

- Neurosexism refers broadly to the ways in which gender roles and claims of sex differences in the brain inform one another. Some feminists have provided a lively critique of the claims of neurosexism, both historically and in recent years, that make for a captivating read.
- The 'case study' of neurosexism allows you to see how feminist social psychologists have attempted to rethink and reappraise some of the taken-for-granted norms of mainstream psychology. We will continue throughout this book to give you other examples of how feminists have 'made trouble' for these kinds of assumptions!

Challenging the validity of sex difference research

According to a meta-analysis (a review of a large number of studies) of sex differences in impulsivity, 'Men engage in impulsive and risky behaviors more frequently than women' (Cross, Copping, & Campbell, 2011, p. 97). The paper clearly demonstrates that the experimental social psychology approach to the topic is still alive and kicking! All the papers reviewed assumed that men were, indeed, naturally more impulsive than women. This is despite the finding that when research like this began in the 1970s on these so-called differences, they turned out to be pretty trivial and highly inconsistent. From that time the empirical evidence showed that women and men are much more alike than they are different, with a great deal of overlap between them (Maccoby and Jacklin, 1974).

Even Cross and her colleagues (2013) report that while men showed significantly higher sensation-seeking, the differences were more modest in relation to effortful control. The big issue is that they conclude that the data reviewed support evolutionary and biological theories of risk-taking! As the data consist of self-reports of one's own behaviour, can we really accept that they somehow provide accurate measurements of *biological* functioning? Cynically, we could ask whether maybe there was some bravado and even machismo involved in the way men describe themselves!

The best way to explain this continued preoccupation with sex differences is to attribute it to straightforward misogyny; that the assumptions being made were and are very biased, arising from the conviction that men and women not only differ, but that women are systematically worse, less-than, or lacking when compared with men. Look at the research in the textbooks you have studied or are studying, and you will see that somehow the agenda has been about demonstrating male superiority. We chose the study cited above to show you how, even when research focuses on male dysfunction, it does so in a way that glamorises propensities like driving too fast.

A feminist question?

As pointed out in Chapter 3, Rhoda Unger may not have been the first to interrogate the preoccupation with sex differences but, by getting her paper published in the prestigious magazine the *American Psychologist* in 1979, she got social psychologists to sit up and really take notice:

> The questions of sex differences ... do not, of themselves, illuminate the mechanisms that create such differences. In fact, they may obscure the origin of such differences by leading us to believe that biological explanations are sufficient for understanding these behaviors. (Unger, 1979, p. 1089)

In her paper, she identifies five key problems with these notions, ones that can have serious political and social impact.

1 The evidence for 'sex differences' is poor. It is questionnaire-based, consisting of self-report data. Sample sizes were often worryingly low and the data obtained varied a lot – by age, social class, and ethnicity. Moreover, the data are distinctly dodgy! For a start, male experimenters were frequently getting different results compared with female experimenters. Unger concludes, 'A variable with this much variety would seem to be an unlikely candidate for one with a biological basis' (1979, p. 1086).

2 The whole concept of 'sex differences' implies a *biological* basis whereby, say, the impulsiveness of boys and men is pre-determined by their

'chromosomes, genes and hormones' (p. 1085). It is seen as something they are naturally born with and cannot change, obscuring the influence of upbringing and all sorts of other social and cultural forces.

3 When 'sex differences' were found, they were frequently used as an *explanation* rather than a description of what is going on, and one that strongly implies – if not directly claims – biological causality. Reasons for the differences are generally looked for in the central nervous system. Unger puts it bluntly: 'psychological theory suggests a direct hook-up between the gonads and the brain' (p.1088). What kind of nonsense is that?

4 While men and women generally agree about what maleness and femaleness are like, Unger argues that it is not biological destinies but societies and cultures that create these expectations.

5 Unger highlights the way that biologically determinist theorists assume that social environments are largely similar for men and women, and avoid exploring what she calls 'environmental factors' (i.e. the socio-cultural environments) – such as the toys children are given to play with from a very early age, the kinds of praise they get, and what they are told not to do.

See and hear for yourself

Go back to the textbooks and/or papers you studied or are currently studying on sex differences. Look for examples of two of Unger's critiques: Critique 2 (inferring that the differences found had a biological basis) and Critique 3 (treating the differences as an explanation). Has Unger convinced you? Discuss with others if you can. Then write some notes reflecting on what you have learned and, crucially, the implications for feminist social psychology.

SECTION SUMMARY

- In Chapter 3, we introduced you to one of the greats of feminist social psychology: Professor Rhoda Unger, who has provided mainstream psychology with plenty to think about over the years. Now you know a lot more about her ideas.
- Sex difference research has been used to justify (or even *evidence*) gender roles or norms, in a problematic way. Feminist social psychologists have made real progress in offering an alternative view of this very biological, essentialist view of difference.

Sex differences and shoddy science

Given the extent to which sex difference research informs our brain-body inferences, social organisation, and gender roles, it should at least be good science, surely! However, the *robustness* of sex difference research has been questioned by feminist psychologists for decades (e.g. Weisstein, 1973). Therefore, there may now be value in utilising the new tools available to feminist researchers to scrutinise the claims of hard-wired sex differences and put the emphasis on the empiricism of lived experience (D'Ignazio & Klein, 2020).

Earlier attempts to reappraise some of the core sex difference work was conducted at a time when the contribution of critical meta-research to psychology was not valued. However, in recent years, psychology has put reproducibility (i.e. the ability for researchers to reproduce the same findings with the same data) and replicability (i.e. the ability to replicate the same results using new data) at the forefront of its research agenda, and an increasing number of voices are re-evaluating the ways in which data are being put to use (D'Ignazio & Klein, 2020).

The Open Science revolution

Open Science is a new paradigm in psychology research that offers new and innovative strategies to examine the robustness (or, in simpler terms, the scientific quality) of research methodology, design, and data. This movement is particularly relevant for us as feminists; the shift in values that Open Science has prompted allows us to reappraise and scrutinise the claims of innate sex differences and biological essentialism in the psychological literature. As we learned in Chapter 2, extensive bias is embedded in psychological research, particularly social psychology research. Therefore, the idea of a true and fully objective finding has become a bit of a tricky sell. And the bias doesn't end there! Problematically, research also shows that those 'positive' findings that paint a neat picture of supported hypotheses and significant results are far more likely to be published in psychology journals, than messy, unsupported, 'null' results. Publishers of psychology research are biased towards significant results that tell a nice persuasive story.

UNDERSTANDING REPLICATION AND REPRODUCIBILITY

So, what is reliability in mainstream social psychology research? Believe it or not, you can learn a lot about the idea of reliable science from The Great British Bake Off (or British Baking Show).

Every week in the Bake Off tent, a group of eager aspirant home bakers are tasked with a 'Technical Challenge'. They each receive the same set of vague baking instructions and a set of ingredients. The challenge here is to *reproduce* the cake, flan, dessert, or pie as closely as possible, with the help of the (deliberately) rather scant recipe provided by the judges. If you've watched any Bake Off episodes, you will know that the Technical Challenge is often a bit of a car crash. Soufflés sink, cakes burn, and there are 'soggy bottoms' aplenty. On the whole, there are usually some pretty fundamental problems with the *reproducibility* of the method; that is, two people working from the same recipe, with seemingly identical ingredients, are not able to reproduce the same results. When we translate this baking analogy into social psychology, the scant recipe is the 'methods' section of a published paper and the end product is the study's results.

In theory, social psychology research should produce reproducible results, i.e. researchers studying prejudice or conflict or group relations in two different laboratories should be able to reproduce the same results when using the same method. On some occasions, as recent reproductivity attempts have shown, the results are picture-perfect. More often than not, though, researchers fail to reproduce the core findings of the original work.

A landmark paper in 2015 threw the field of social psychology into panicked disarray. A team of psychologists, the **Open Science Collaboration**, clubbed together in an attempt to estimate the reliability of 100 of psychology's most influential empirical studies. In the original 100 studies, 97% reported significant results. Of the replication attempts, only 36% did so. This one paper sent ripples throughout the field, prompting a new variant of social psychology that centres on the reproducibility and replicability of results.

ACTIVITY 6.3: Feminist psychology and replication

Although the extent to which feminist research questions can be asked within this scientific paradigm, mainstream social psychology is firmly at the centre of this model. There are inherent tensions between 'reliability' of psychology research and the biases that are inherent at every stage of the process. If we are to take the conventions of science seriously, then, at the very least, 'psychological science' should be reproducible, reliable, and replicable. These concepts have been thrust onto psychology's agenda in recent years.

Given everything we discussed earlier in this chapter about the celebration of bias in different ways, take some time to reflect upon how this informs conversations about replication attempts in feminist psychology. You may wish to consider the following questions:

- If feminist psychology, as we have talked about it throughout this book, is concerned with lived experience, research positionality, situatedness, and subjectivity, do you think this is at odds with the moves towards 'reproducibility'?
- What additional challenges may feminist psychologists have to account for in moves to make feminist research more open and transparent?
- Would you expect feminist research to directly replicate, much like the mainstream experimental work? If not, why not?

Concerns with sex difference research

Whether or not feminist social psychological research fits neatly into the Open Science movement agenda is part of a larger conversation. However, the

Open Science revolution can be useful to feminist psychologists, as it provides us with a set of 'rigour criteria' and, perhaps more importantly, a *vocabulary* with which to articulate our concerns. In a paper that I (M.P.) wrote recently with Sofia Persson, we stress that Open Science and feminist psychology can join forces to dismantle some of the problematic claims in the neurosexist literature. Our core concerns of sex difference research, particularly related to the claims of objectivity, are summarised below:

Replication concerns

If research is to be robust and reliable, researchers should be able to directly and conceptually replicate its core findings. This should particularly be the case with research that has lofty claims of innate sex differences between men and women, given how these claims are used to determine social roles, expectations, and opportunities. As you will have read in the *Feminism & Psychology* special issue, some feminist scholars, such as Janet Shibley Hyde, have long expressed concerns over the overall lack of replication attempts in sex difference research.

For experimental, quantitative research, the Open Science movement suggests that we can only really know if a phenomenon is 'true' or robust if researchers are able to conduct the same study with different participants and obtain the same result. If a finding doesn't replicate, chances are it's either (a) a fluke (or false positive, or 'type 1 error'), or (b) only relevant to the very specific testing contexts and population of the original study.

Replication attempts in relation to sex difference research are the first step in combatting the pervasiveness of neurosexism (Persson & Pownall, 2021). Alice Eagly has advocated for robust and reliable methods in this research, as they allow us to uncover non-significant or 'null' findings in the literature. This challenges the 'difference bias' that pervades the literature, whereby we are far more interested in finding difference than we are finding non-significant evidence for similarities between groups.

Publication bias

Overwhelmingly, investigations into sex comparisons of the brain show evidence of *difference* (see our earlier discussion about 'difference bias'!) and very few studies provide evidence for similarities. However, given the principles of probability and chance, and the messiness of psychological data, in theory, even if 'true' effects existed, there should be some studies that inevitably demonstrate null effects, even if these are also errors or 'flukes'. Gina Rippon (2019), who has been instrumental in challenging shoddy sex difference claims, calls this kind of bias 'selective publication', whereby non-significant results, which have the potential to contradict or challenge previous popular findings, are 'hidden away – the file drawer problem!

To add to this, it is difficult to challenge sex difference claims because they have popular appeal, provide 'sexy' headline-grabbing conclusions, and intuitively seem to 'make sense' (Fine, 2012). Ruti (2015) has suggested that the popularity of neurosexism stems from the notion that it generally confirms our view of the world, rather than challenging it (see 'confirmation bias' in Chapter 2 for more on this). More broadly, this means that data which contradict popularised notions of hard-wired brain differences between the sexes is dropped, hidden away, or (even worse) massaged and manipulated to create nice, neat significant results (Chambers, 2019).

Questionable research practices

Although it is built upon claims of being objective and detached, the Open Science movement has demonstrated how quantitative data can be 'tortured to confess to anything' (Chambers, 2019, p. 21). The 'undisclosed flexibility' of the way quantitative data is analysed means that there are a multitude of decisions that researchers make in the research process, which ultimately affect its final destination. While researchers will often make these decisions without any malicious intent, conscious and unconscious decisions in the research process can impact the results. W.S.R. was actually taught how to do this by one of her supervisors! These dodgy practices are especially crucial to interrogate in the context of neuroscience, due to the level of mess or 'noise' that exists in neurological studies (head movements, equipment noise, and so on). Because of this, and other concerns about the claims of robustness in neurological studies, it is impossible to draw definitive conclusions about how sex differences inform behaviour.

'Bropen science'

Concern for replication and reproducibility of social psychology's findings should, in theory, trigger a wonderful new wave of diverse, intersectional, and creative approaches to thinking about research. However, it has been criticised for perpetuating inequalities that exist within social psychology more broadly. For example, the White masculine dominance of Open Science movements is ironic and problematic and has led to feminist open scientists coining the phrase 'bropen science' (see Whitaker & Guest, 2020). Bropen science ultimately creates an elitist and exclusive kind of environment, where anyone who is not an (ostensibly) knowledgeable White male is made to feel unwelcome and unable to participate. This is again deeply ironic, given how the point of Open Science is to shift away from academic exclusivity!

As you saw in Chapter 3, *bros* can take multiple forms. Kirstie Whitaker and Olivia Guest (2020) provide a lovely overview of these problems in their article in *The Psychologist*, which you can freely access. We particularly enjoy their 'call to arms' at the end of their discussion, where they stress that 'the only way to dismantle structural and systemic biases is to listen to those who experience them. If you practice lots of aspects of open scholarship, our call to action is to listen to those who do not or cannot. Read what they write, hear what they say, and digest their reasoning. This is how to help them become truly open'.

SECTION SUMMARY

- This section has introduced you to perhaps one of the biggest discussions happening in social psychology at the moment: the Open Science revolution and the rapidly growing concern for replicability and reproducibility.
- Calls for social psychology to improve the rigour and robustness of its methodologies may be fertile ground for feminist approaches to psychology, as the whole discipline is having something of an 'identity crisis'. This provides a useful opportunity to encourage other psychologists to rethink the dominant 'ways of doing' and maybe (we hope!) give way to more feminist approaches.

This chapter has covered a lot of ground. We've talked about Open Science, sex differences, neurosexism, and the sex/gender divide. This all comes under the broad theme of scientific research being heavily dominated by one group of voices, which does not always allow for a critical and diverse account of the human experience. Angela Saini tackles the question of why there is such extreme antagonism among some in the scientific community, and why the case being made in support of a biological explanation is so highly emotionally charged. In her book, *Inferior* (2017), about 'how science got women wrong', Saini conducts a meticulous and well-informed appraisal of the theories developed about how and why women are biologically inferior to men. She systematically demonstrates the faulty logic and poor research practices that have led to these conclusions. We like the way Hartmunt Böhme put it when he wrote that this sort of theorising is 'nothing more than machismo masquerading as theory' (2014, p. 13).

CHAPTER SUMMARY

- In this chapter, we have taken one particularly harmful anti-feminist idea in the psychological literature and we have assessed the ways in which it can be challenged and discussed in feminist social spaces.
- This chapter has covered the replication crisis that social psychology is currently firmly in the midst of and has demonstrated the ways that 'Open Science' and feminist methodologies may have a lot to inform one another about.
- This chapter has also prompted you to consider whether you think replication and reproducibility are, or rather *should be*, goals of feminist psychology research, as well as mainstream social psychology work.

7 Communication and language

Learning objectives

Study of this chapter (including its activities) should enable you to:

- Recognise the importance of communication in feminist social psychology – our work in this field has been instrumental to the development of theory, research evidence and, in particular, feminist methods.
- Gain insight into how non-verbal communication functions, its power to engender emotion, and the subtlety with which it operates.
- Recognise that early social psychologists assumed that women's language consists of lots of polite talk about trivial things, whereas men's language consists of measured and logical talk about important things. Lies, lies, neither is true!
- Realise that in societies based on patriarchy, women have to cope with using a man-made language – developed and policed by men from a male perspective and often inadequate or inappropriate to serve women's interests and purposes.
- Understand some of the ways in which men can deploy language strategically to deny their agency and hence responsibility for their actions.
- Gain knowledge about Conversational Analysis (CA) as a means to reveal such strategies in operation.
- Gain insight into how feminist social psychologists are now challenging and changing 'received' language use, for example in the ways we write up the results of our research.
- Learn more about the new, postfeminist, sensibility that, in a neoliberal world, is making life tougher for women and girls.

Social psychology is about the ways in which we influence one another within our interactions and relationships with each other – as partners, families, peer groups, co-workers, and communities; and about who we are – as mothers, friends, managers, citizens (or not), students, and pensioners, as well as all the other social roles we can (or cannot) adopt. And all of this is only possible because we communicate with each other in multiple different ways. In this chapter, we will explore the impact of feminist theorisation and research on the role that communication plays in social action and interaction. Studying language and other representational systems is incredibly important to feminist social psychology, since its focus is on how we both construct meaning and have it constructed for us. Furthermore, the English language (like most languages) is very much a product of **patriarchy**, constructed through men talking *to* men and writing *for* other men and agreeing on its grammar, structure, and content.

Non-verbal communication

Body language complements and reinforces talk, making effective communication easier to accomplish. We can get clues about whether the other person is being honest by looking at their body language. Even when people control what they say and the way they speak, so that they *sound* as if they are being genuine, their gestures and stance can give them away. What interests social psychologists in particular are the social and cultural conventions – called display rules – that control the way people communicate, for instance, specific kinds of emotion to each other. For example, in northern Europe and Asia men, in particular, have been expected to 'damp down' emotional expression whereas women are expected to be more open about their emotions (though not in professional settings). Smiling is an emotional expression that is 'required' of women. In certain jobs – mainly those serving customers – women staff in particular are required to appear charming and cheerful, irrespective of what they may be feeling inside. Such work is called emotional labour, pointing to the effort involved in presenting a cheery face for hours on end, however obnoxiously the customers are behaving.

Gaze and eye contact

Gaze, in this context, refers to the time spent looking directly at another person. Eye contact refers to mutual gaze, when people 'catch each other's eyes'. Both are extensively used to communicate – to signal status, to signal interest and sincerity, to manage conversations, and to exert control. The 'proper' use of gaze in conversations varies by cultural conventions and is usually powerfully gendered. For example, in many cultures people in subordinate positions are expected to keep their eyes lowered when speaking to a superior. Note that for women this can be their father or husband as well as their boss. In this way, female deference to men is, literally, 'written on their bodies'.

Sociologists call this **habitus**; it is the way in which we learn to deploy our body in ways that are appropriate for our gender, social status, and so on. In pretty well all cultures, the social rules about eye contact are highly gendered. Transgressing them can be very disturbing. A woman who uses 'inappropriately' powerful levels of eye contact, even today, will come across as 'lacking femininity', as 'difficult' and 'unnatural'; she will be perceived as being 'incredibly bossy' and lacking respect. The point being made here (by someone who has been called all of those names and much worse) is just how deeply patriarchy is embedded in our habitus, woven as it is into the way we interpret something as 'natural' as glances and looks. This is an excellent example of the way **sexism** can be unintended and unconscious, and yet still very powerful in its impact. Interpersonal distance is another illustration – think just how intimidating it can be when someone 'invades' your personal space.

Some of the simplest features of non-verbal communication are on view when someone is using eye contact to impose dominance – or to resist it, such as by refusing to acknowledge somebody who is seeking to interject within a conversation. A good way to study this is to watch people converse – in a meeting, say, or a group of friends chatting to each other over a meal. Psychologists have conducted vast amounts of research on what goes on, and almost always men come out best in the conversational dominance game (see Stokoe, 2000).

Paralinguistics is also important here – the ums and ahs, the inflexions in a voice, pauses and interruptions, all convey meaning and add subtle nuance to what is being said. Social psychologists, as you will see later in the chapter, can use these elements to interpret a lot about what is going on in a conversation, using what is called 'conversational analysis'.

SECTION SUMMARY

- Non-verbal communication is the product of a person's habitus – the way they have learned to stand, sit, walk, gesture, and make eye contact in appropriate ways for their gender, social status, etc. It is therefore largely unconscious.
- It can be very powerful, particularly in communicating emotion – generating joy, excitement, fear, and social discomfort.
- In most cultures, boys are brought up to express dominance and entitlement in the way they communicate non-verbally, girls to express deference and humility.
- Breaking these rules as a girl or woman can be very uncomfortable – it is often read as 'unnatural' and in a negative manner. Breaking them as a boy or man is also discomforting – getting branded as a 'sissy' and subjected to ridicule. Today, though, there are accepted ways of being 'performatively gay' deliberately.
- Language is not just about the words said, its paralinguistic features also convey a great deal of information.

Troubles with language and gender

Early social psychology took the same old essentialist approach to the ways in which language is gendered – it spent its time and energy spelling out the failures and inadequacies of women when compared with men. A good example is the work of Robin Talmoch Lakoff. In her book *Language and Woman's Place* (2004), first published in 1975, she set out her perception of 'women's language', how and why it is dysfunctional, and how women can be helped to change how they speak, and thereby get taken more seriously. She described women's speech style as overly polite, overly grammatical, hesitant, and ingratiating, full of empty adjectives and irritating 'tag' questions. She concluded that women can't tell jokes and have no sense of humour. Yet Lakoff presented very little empirical evidence for her claims. Her approach was largely one of introspection. Even so, her work was enormously influential, well outside her own discipline (linguistics), including on social psychology. It led to a flurry of experimental studies, all seeking to confirm or reject the concept of a distinctly womanly speech style.

Being forced to use men's language

As a direct challenge to Lakoff, for her PhD Dale Spender studied the extent to which language is 'man-made'. In her subsequent book, *Man Made Language*, first published in 1980, Spender argued that patriarchal societies are fundamentally based on the conviction that males are superior to females, and that its social practices function to *make* this belief 'come true'. In particular, she claims, patriarchies construct languages that favour boys and men and denigrate girls and women. In the UK, she said, to use the 'Queen's English' is to have no choice but to collude with this bias. The consequence, Spender argues, is that women 'remain "outsiders", borrowers of the language ... that men have made ... [T]his monopoly over language is one of the means by which males have ensured their own primacy' (1985, p. 12).

A good illustration is to compare categories of people in relation to gender:

Male	Female
Governor	Governess
Major	Majorette
Courtier	Courtesan
Master	Mistress
Bachelor	Spinster
Maestro	Prima Donna
Steward	Stewardess

For a start, notice that the difference between the terms 'male' and 'female' often entails the addition of a couple of letters, treating the male version as the norm and the female version as 'male-not'. From this point on, the female words are *'perjurated'*; that is, they are made negative, smaller, or more trivial, often with a salacious undercurrent implying sexual wantonness! As pointed out by two feminist scholars, Casey Miller and Kate Swift, 'once a name or a word becomes associated with women, it is rarely again considered suitable for males' (1976, p. 6). A good illustration here is the observation that, in the US, boy's names such as Shirley, Leslie, Beverley, Evelyn, and Sidney stopped being seen as suitable for boys as soon as parents started to call their daughters by them! It is worth noting that Julia Stanley estimated that while the English language has many more names for males than females, it has 220 words for sexually promiscuous women and just 20 for promiscuous males (Stanley, 1973).

He/Man Language

As an undergraduate in the 1960s, I (W.S.R.) remember complaining to the lecturers that I had real problems reading the textbooks they set me, as they kept talking about 'man' and 'mankind' as if these words function as generic terms for all humans. I simply could not relate to being called 'he' and 'him'. Here's an example from a textbook on social psychology at that time:

> In this chapter we shall take as our abstract human being with which his independent self-hood, his capacities for doing the sort of things that human beings can do: perceive with his various senses, reason, have standards of conduct, and consider the sorts of social influences to which he is subjected. (Sprott, 1952)

You can see my problem! Right into the 1970s and even later, psychology textbooks followed the rule that, grammatically, 'man embraces woman'. At that time, all my lecturers in the Psychology Department were men. Somewhat pompously they replied that the books were simply grammatically correct. I do remember muttering, subversively, that it was men who invented the grammar – yes, I was a feminist even then (I thank my mother). But I didn't make a fuss.

Spender (1985) offers a helpful history of how this trick was pulled off. She traces its origin to a Mr Wilson in 1553, who wrote that it was 'more natural to place man before woman'. He was writing for an almost exclusively male audience, who, unsurprisingly, all agreed with him. Spender comments that the 'seal was set on male superiority … when in 1746 John Kirkby formulated his "Eighty Eight Grammatical Rules" … Rule Twenty One stated that the male gender was *more comprehensive* than the female' (1985, p.148, emphasis in the original). Arbitrarily converting maleness into a universal category is a highly significant move. It both institutionalised male bias and made the English language a nightmare for women. But even worse, it simply did not work! An example will help. The famous psychologist Erich Fromm blithely wrote that 'man's "vital interests" were "life, food, access to females etc."', while Loren Eisley penned of man that 'his back aches, he ruptures easily, his women have difficulties in childbirth' (Spender, 1985, p. 155). Not very comprehensive after all, then?

Attempts by women to do something about this problem tended to be sternly rejected, often with great hostility. An example occurred in the 1960s when an attempt was made in the US to address the *he/male* issue by the National Education Association. In their literature and speech to and about elementary (primary) schoolteachers, they began to refer to them as 'she', as the vast majority of them were, indeed, women. Yet male members of the Association became very angry, stating that doing so 'was responsible for their poor public image and consequently their low salaries'. At their Assembly, a male delegate attacked the woman who was speaking, decrying her 'incorrect and improper use of the English language' and stating that 'the interests of neither women or men ... are served by grammatical usage which conjures up an anachronistic image of the nineteenth century school marm' (Miller and Swift, 1976, p. 430).

SECTION SUMMARY

- In the 1960s and 1970s, social psychologists still regarded women's use of language as inferior to the way men used it. Dale Spender challenged this assumption, arguing that the English language (alongside many other languages of course) is a product of patriarchy, *designed* to give men many advantages over women. Not surprisingly, women have difficulties in making it work for them.

- Male grammarians invented rules that categorised maleness as comprehensive – humankind became mankind, and people in general were universally referred to as he/him.

- Feminist social psychologists have developed a number of strategies for challenging the way language has been used, and are devising ways to make changes to resolve the inconsistencies and bias.

Challenging patriarchal language

Mary Crawford (1995) adopted a cleverly disparaging term to describe the popular books that have been written around the idea that women and men talk and think in different languages – 'bandwagon books'. They include Deborah Tannen's (1990) *You Just Don't Understand* and, perhaps the best known of the genre, John Gray's (1992) *Men are from Mars, Women are from Venus*. Danielle Popp and her colleagues (including Mary Crawford) sum up the general message being sent out by books like this very well: 'men are believed to have demanding voices; to be dominating, authoritarian, straight to the point, blunt, forceful, aggressive, boastful, militant; and to use swear words and slang. Women are believed to use good grammar and enunciate clearly; to speak politely, gently, rapidly, and emotionally; to talk a lot; to talk about trivial topics; and to indulge in gossip and gibberish' (Popp et al., 2003, p. 318). Dale Spender put it all rather more succinctly: 'In short, feminine talk is a lot of polite talk about silly things; whereas masculine talk is a little blunt talk about important things' (Spender, 1979, quoted in Popp et al., 2003, p. 318). This has become 'popular wisdom' – 'what everybody knows'. This linguistic sexism needs to change and feminist social psychologists have used a number of analytic approaches to tease out some of the ways in which sexism, dominance, and oppression operate within male language.

Language directly used to deny agency

Social psychology has drawn on theorisation from many other disciplines to approach the interplay between gender and language in a more nuanced way. A good example is the work of the feminist political scientist, Jill Vickers, who drew attention to the way that, when men speak and, especially, when they write, they frequently deny their own agency: they use a language strategy by which they deny any responsibility for the things they do and fail to do (Vickers, 1982). For example, men often describe their aggression towards women as 'teasing', claiming it is a 'joke' – and accusing them of 'not having a sense of humour'. Yet they dissemble and this needs to be exposed. Crawford points out, for example, a list of jokes about women for which there are no parallels: 'prostitute jokes, mother-in-law jokes, dumb blonde jokes, women driver jokes, Jewish mother jokes' (Crawford, 1995, p. 138). For women in general, these are not at all funny, especially when you fit the category that is being ridiculed.

But it is more serious than that. Vickers said that denying agency is 'the worst kind of context stripping ... a grammatical, theoretical and methodological trick' (1982, p. 39) that beguiles the reader or listener into colluding with the misattributed agency. Masculine linguistic strategies like this are often used to obscure, deny, and to reverse agency – that is, their language strategy is a clever and effective form of *gaslighting*. Often it is unconscious – it is how boys have been taught and encouraged to express themselves, an action so over-learned it has become automatic and unconscious in adulthood. However, Vickers was particularly concerned about the way that the objectivist language adopted by scientific and other 'masculine' writing can be used to obscure who is doing what to whom. Vickers illustrated her case with the following statement (cited by Daly) about *suttee* – this is the 'custom' or 'practice' in which Hindu widows throw themselves on their husband's funeral pyres. She quotes a description taken from a textbook about Hinduism:

> At first, suttee was restricted to the wives of princes and warriors ... but in the course of time the widows of weavers, masons, barbers and others of the lower caste *adopted the practice*. (Walker, cited in Daly 1978, p. 771, emphasis added by Daly)

In her paper, Vickers responded:

> Given the fact that widows were dragged from hiding places and heavily drugged before being flung on the pyre, often by their sons, this is like saying that although the practice of being burned in gas ovens was at first restricted to political dissidents, eventually millions of Jews *adopted the practice*. (1982, p. 39, emphasis in the original).

ACTIVITY 7.1

Now you are alert to language being used in this way, keep a watch out for it over the next few weeks. Look for it in particular in the reports you read about social psychology research. Note how it actively seeks to distance the researcher from any responsibility for or ethical engagement in what is going on. The aim here is to make you more wary and cautious, suspicious even, about what some social psychologists want you to believe.

Challenging 'Just say no!'

In the 1980s and 1990s, many universities and colleges sought to deal with sexual harassment by offering women training in how to tackle unwanted advances from men. Feminist scholars objected, arguing that it was the *men* who needed training to stop them behaving in a predatory manner. Two feminist psychologists, Celia Kitzinger and Hannah Frith (1999), made their case, based on conversational analysis research on the paralinguistic differences between accepting an invitation, and refusing one. Conversational analysis is a qualitative technique whereby naturally occurring conversations are recorded and transcribed, and then subjected to careful scrutiny of their paralanguage elements in order to understand 'what is going on' in the conversation.

To make sense of their data, you will need to get to know some of the conventions used in conversational analysis for annotating text. These notations allow information about things like pauses, talking over each other, and so on to be subjected to analysis.

Conversation analysis transcription notations

[	overlapping speech
:	sound is drawn out (the more :::, the longer the drawing out)
(.)	pause of less than 0.2 seconds
(0.2)	pause measured in seconds
text	emphasis
.hhh	in-breath (the more hhh, the longer the in-breath)
hhh	out-breath (the more hhh, the longer the out-breath)
=	no pause
,	slight rising intonation

Note: It can help to actually say out loud what was being said, feeding in the pauses and the words that are stretched or mumbled.

Kitzinger and Frith begin their paper by pointing out that refusing a request tends to be much harder to pull off than agreeing. To demonstrate this, they first gave examples of how an agreement tends to work:

Example 1 (Atkinson & Drew, 1979, p. 58)
A: Why don't you come up and see me some[time
B: [I would like to.

Example 2 (Davidson, 1984, p. 116)
A: We:ll, will you help me [ou:t
B: [I certainly wi:ll.

Overlapping speech like these examples are typical of the immediate and direct way that someone agrees to a request.

Kitzinger and Frith contrast this with an example of an everyday refusal:

Example 3 (Potter & Wetherell, 1987, p. 86)
Mark: We were wondering if you wanted to come over Saturday, f'r dinner
(0.4 sec pause)
Jane: Well (.) .hh it'd be great but we promised Carol already.

Far from being immediate and direct, this refusal is slow to be given and hedged around. There is a 0.4 second gap before Jane starts speaking, and another pause – indicated by (.) – after she uses 'Well' as a hedge. A 'hedge' (sometimes called a preface) is a word or utterance like 'uh' at the start of speech, used to 'hedge around' difficulties to come. Then Jane uses a palliative – here it is an attempt to 'sweeten the blow' – to specifically ameliorate the potential rudeness of rejecting the invitation. Palliatives are conversational strategies used to temper the impact of what is being said. They are often used in rejections: 'That's awfully sweet of you, but', 'I would love to, but', and so on. Finally, Jane provides an 'account' – here a justification for refusing the invitation. Accounts like these present culturally sanctioned reasons for acting (or not acting) in particular ways. In refusals, accounts convey the rationale that the person cannot (as opposed to will not or does not want to) agree to the request. Their purpose is to avoid the implication that the request is unreasonable or unattractive, and so avoid negative consequences for the relationship between the speakers.

Having used the fine-grained qualities of conversation analysis to make the point that refusals are generally problematic – and hence usually presented in ambiguous and hedged ways – Kitzinger and Frith turn their attention to the way people generally react to such refusals.

Example 4 (Davidson, 1984, p. 113)
A: hhhhh Uh will you call 'im tuhnight for me, =
B: = eYea:h
      (.)
A: Plea::se,

In this example it is clear that the person asking the favour has recognised they are not getting the kind of definite, swift agreement that means that B has actually agreed to make the 'phone call. So A responds by making a more powerful plea – 'Plea::se'. Kitzinger and Frith provide a number of similar examples to show that people generally have no problem whatsoever in recognising refusals, even when they are tacit and vague and sometimes include hedged or even apparent agreement. They take action accordingly, for instance, by (as above) asking again more persuasively, seeking to reassure, or to counter the excuse being given.

Kitzinger and Frith then come to the main point of their article, which is to counter the explanations usually given – that it is simply a matter of miscommunication when men make inappropriate sexual advances towards women. It has been attributed to women 'lacking effective refusal skills' (Cairns, 1993, p. 205), in a context in which 'often men interpret timidity as permission' (cited in Turner & Rubinson, 1993, p. 605). These attributions, Kitzinger and Frith argue, locate the problem (i.e. the agency) in women's communicational competence rather than in anything that men do or don't do. Using their fine-grained analysis of refusals in ordinary settings, Kitzinger and Frith dispute this explanation, and maintain that the problem should be located in men's behaviour: 'Our analysis in this article supports the belief that the root of the problem is not that men do not *understand* sexual refusals, but they do not *like* them' (Kitzinger & Frith, 1999, p. 310, emphasis added).

The authors marshal a raft of further evidence to support their case. For example, when posters were put up on a university campus in Canada saying 'No means No', some men responded with posters of their own. The captions demonstrate incredible levels of hostility: 'No means kick her in the teeth', 'No means on your knees bitch', 'No means tie her up', and 'No means more beer' (Mahood & Littlewood 1997).

Kitzinger and Frith's article demonstrates how conversation analysis can be used by feminist social psychologists to examine how meaning is often interpreted not from the semantic qualities of language but the subtle paralinguistic ways in which it is deployed. The article also shows how, within a social constructionist paradigm, a number of different sources of data can be used together to address the way language is used strategically – for example, to warrant certain kinds of behaviour.

SECTION SUMMARY

- Feminist social psychologists have developed a number of strategies for changing and challenging the way patriarchal language is being deployed to cover up misbehaviour.
- Vickers demonstrated how men justify and cover up their violence by calling it a 'custom' (such as suttee) that is presented as ethically neutral when it is clearly not.
- Kitzinger and Frith used conversational analysis to demonstrate that it is not that women are incapable of refusing properly, but that men pretend they don't recognise refusals, when they are perfectly obvious.

Communication within a post-feminist world

So, what has changed, now we live in a post-feminist world? Ros Gill suggests that *post-feminism* (or post-sexism) is a 'distinctive sensibility' (2007, p. 147), which brings together a number of strands: the belief that femininity is a property of women's *bodies*, that bodily femininity demands high levels of self-monitoring and self-discipline to achieve, and that it is an individual choice, freely made, to do so. Gill views this sensibility as a reaction *against* feminism, within a *neoliberal* system where life is viewed as a competition in which there are 'winners' and 'losers' (and, after all, nobody wants to be a loser). Gill sees this interconnected set of ideas as constructed through depictions in the mass and social media, including films, TV programmes, selfies and the reactions to them, such as 'likes' and comments on FaceBook, TikTok, and Twitter. Gill cautions that we must not regard post-feminism as a historical development *on from* feminism, or as a simple backlash, but as a new social phenomenon that is worthy of study itself.

Just between girls

Sarah Riley, Adrienne Evans, and Alison Mackiewicz (2016) have explored the ways in which, within a post-feminist setting, young women talk about the way they look at each other. In earlier times, feminist scholarship focused on the impact of the '*male gaze*' – the way that women were seen and saw themselves from a male perspective. As we saw in Chapter 6, the dominance of the male gaze in films and TV created a blueprint for what constitutes desirable femininity, one which *objectifies* women – literally viewing women *solely* as the objects of men's desire. Objectification like this strips women of their ability to define themselves, and forces them into a patriarchal straightjacket.

By shifting focus to the 'female gaze' (how women look at and judge each other), Riley and her colleagues were able to explore women's subjectivity – that is, the selfhood they construct for themselves. This process Riley et al. call 'subject formation' (another term for subject positioning – see Chapter 3). While this may appear liberating, sadly it is not. There are other subject positions knocking around to entrap them. Nikolas Rose's notion of *governmentality* (Rose, O'Malley, & Valverde, 2006) is useful here (see Chapter 3). It refers to the insidious power that is exercised through convincing people that they are free to choose how to live their lives but creates the conditions under which they are forced to discipline *themselves*; Anne-Marie Mol, a Dutch philosopher asserts that, under neoliberalism, people 'have to control, tame and transcend their bodies so as to be able to choose' (2008, p. 40).

According to Riley and her colleagues, for young women, this is currently driven by 'an appearance-related, consumer-oriented looking' (2016, p. 95); what Angela McRobbie (2009) calls '*hyper-feminine forms of consumption*'. It is where women are presented with a gamut of technologies, products, and services to help them to 'improve' their looks: skin bleaching for being too coloured/ tanning for being too pale; waxing and shaving to control body hair; manicures to make fingernails ornamental. These are promoted as essential for any self-respecting young woman, because, as we are told, we are worth it! Today, acceptable female identities require women (not just young ones) to comply with all this; nobody must think you have 'let yourself go'. Riley et al. draw attention to the way this largely reflects a white, middle-class aesthetic (see Ringrose & Walkerdine, 2008). Not that this goes uncontested – Gentles-Peart (2020) describes how Black Caribbean women in the US have formed friendship groups to resist the colonisation that has dehumanised their bodies, and, instead, to celebrate the voluptuous joy of their 'thick black bodies'.

Riley and her colleagues (2016) conducted semi-structured interviews with two cohorts of young women for their research on 'looking talking': one with women aged 18–27 years who got involved in the UK night-time economy, going out drinking with each other; and the other with 23–35-year-olds engaging in new sexual subjectivities. The two locations were selected because they were social spaces within which the post-feminist sensibility is enacted, and where the talk in question was 'just between girls'. The analysis (as with most feminist research) is subtle and nuanced, but some key findings were:

1 Looking talk between women is generally seen to be judgemental and competitive, even between good friends, who were expected to be kinder to each other but were not. This was seen as making women distressed and hence as problematic.
2 The women expressed nostalgia for the times when all you needed to do was look good for the boys, who had less exacting standards. They say life was easier then, when their self-esteem was not under attack.
3 These very high standards of appearance set by women were perceived as too demanding in terms of how long it takes to get ready in the morning, how much it costs, and how the constant surveillance from other women puts pressure on them to conform.
4 The pressure is consumer-focused, so that, say, they have stopped enjoying being pampered and have started to feel edgy, overstretched, and tense all the time.
5 Women today feel more vulnerable and pressured to conform.

SECTION SUMMARY

- Post-feminism is best understood as a new sensibility – a phenomenon in itself, not just a phase following on from feminism or a backlash against it. Its origins are in the increasing foregrounding of neoliberalism, which is powerfully driven by commercial forces and the ascendancy of the profit motive.
- An example of what is going on is the shift from the dominance of the 'male gaze' to a situation where the 'female gaze' becomes more influential.
- Heterosexual femininity is increasingly understood as a consumer-orientated bodily practice, operated through judgemental looking between women.

In this chapter, we have exposed how many years of patriarchy have undermined women's ability to speak for themselves and resist being silenced. Feminist social psychologists have very effectively challenged the misogyny built into all forms of communication, but in particular language. Challenge like this can give us a sense of just how much needs to be changed if women's concerns are to be addressed and their interests properly attended to. At least we are now finding ways to pull aside the veils that cover up how patriarchal power gets exercised to 'keep us in our place'.

CHAPTER SUMMARY

- People influence each other through communicating with one another. So, for feminists, knowing about the chicanery going on is crucial for us to improve how women are treated and what they can achieve.
- Non-verbal communication (including paralanguage) is very powerful, especially for signalling the subtleties of dominance and submission, emotions and feelings, by which women are intimidated.
- Language itself is a particularly potent means of communication because of its capacity to convey information.
- The impact of patriarchy on both of these communication systems has created deeply embedded mechanisms by which dominant males can control and regulate.
- The better we get at undermining them, the more we can achieve. Onwards and upwards!

8 Roles and relationships

Learning objectives

Study of this chapter (including its activities) should enable you to:

- Cast a critical feminist eye over claims of evolutionary psychology on romantic relationships and attractiveness, which generally position women as passive and men as active.
- Understand how evolutionary ideas about men and women in romantic relationships may contribute to the infantilisation of women.
- Get to grips with some of the core problems with mainstream relationship research, such as 'compulsory cisgenderism', 'heteronormativity', and the promotion of hegemonic masculinity.
- Learn more about feminist work on friendship, particularly female friendship.
- Understand how relationships and friendships are often played out against a backdrop of neoliberalism and 'post-sexism'.
- Critically appreciate the complex and nuanced literature that demonstrates how the role of mother is entrenched with gendered inequalities and social constructions, making it a hotbed of feminist ideas!

A feminist understanding of romantic relationships

Feminists have historically advocated for a critical and creative reappraisal of most elements of the human experience, as we have discussed throughout this Companion. Now it's time for us to turn this critical eye to Tina Turner's immortal question: 'What's love got to do with it?'. As Margaret Wetherell (1995) has argued, the romantic love *discourse is* a device for understanding the significance of feminism and provides a useful opportunity to confront cultural representations or assumptions that have long since troubled feminist psychologists. Wetherell suggests that the discourse of romantic love is a site where many of feminist psychology's concerns culminate. She then explains how the ways in which society frames love, romance, and 'the search for a mate' largely reflect problematic gender norms, assumptions, and stereotypes. For example, she notes that 'in popular culture, women and girls are assigned romantic fiction and boys and men pornography' (1995, p. 133).

According to Katherine Allen and Ana Jaramillo-Sierra (2015), there are four core elements that differentiate feminist approaches from non-feminist ones in the study of relationships:

1 First, gender is treated as the central axis of analysis, and gender is positioned as a 'system of power' that differentiates men and women. In other words, men generally have more power, and women have less.
2 Gender inequality is actively constructed by society and, therefore, it can be demolished too.
3 Gender inequality is wrong and problematic for women.
4 Feminists have a duty to promote social change that 'undoes' gender inequality, and unravel the ways in which it harms individuals, families, and societies (Chafetz, 2004).

Equally important to feminist scholarship is to create the knowledge necessary to change social conditions and advocate for fair and respectful arrangements between men and women living together in families. We need to know how to dismantle the social stratifications of gender, race, class, sexual orientation, age, and the like, since these are the primary ways in which disadvantage and oppression are structured. A good start is to look critically at the assumptions of mainstream research into relationships because, from a feminist perspective, they create an environment that is toxic for the building of good relationships: that is, the imposition of *heteronormativity* and *cisgenderism*.

Heteronormativity

A pervasive problem in the mainstream study of relationships is the expectation of '*compulsory heterosexuality*' or, to use Adrienne Rich's (1980) term, '*heteronormativity*'. This is making the assumption that heterosexual boy-girl relationships are 'the norm' and any relationship different from that is 'Other'. Heteronormativity is thus the assumption that heterosexuality is the normal human condition. We know all about the harms of *Othering* from Chapter 5. Jaqui Gabb and her colleagues at the Open University explored couple relationships in Britain in a survey project they named *Enduring Love*. As you might imagine, they found relationships to be highly diverse and changing, and how contemporary relationships exist in 'increasingly fluid forms, experience and expectations of long-term personal and sexual commitments' (Gabb et al., 2013, p. 74).

Heteronormativity is an idea that derives from *queer theory*, a movement that emerged in the 1990s to recognise as legitimate diverse sexualities across the humanities and social sciences. According to queer theory, heteronormativity means that non-heterosexual people are made a spectacle of and problematised (Herek, 2007). A good illustration in social psychology research is where a recruitment advertisement for a research study *presumes* heterosexuality, or its inclusion criteria *mandate* heterosexuality (Herek et al., 1991). An excellent paper by Thorne, Hegarty, and Hepper (2019) provides a review of the issues with heteronormativity in psychological research on romantic love, and summarises the key concerns brilliantly. The authors also explain how heteronormativity goes beyond assuming that heterosexual equals normal, and show how 'normativity' also relies on certain norms, such as monogamy, reproduction, and marriage:

> Heteronormativity also refers to the normalization of more than heterosexual identity; the assumption that 'normal' healthy relationships must be marital, monogamous, reproductive relationships. These two aspects of heteronormativity interact in a *failure* to notice some same-gender and mixed-gender relationships are different. (Thorne et al., 2019, p. 248)

Beyond the problematic normativity, heterosexual practices have also been thought to socially construct men as active initiators and women as passive receivers, which has been related to sexual coercion in heterosexual relationships (Gavey, 1989).

Cisgenderism

Gender is very complicated and highly context-dependent, as evidenced by certain emic constructs of gender (we talk about this a lot in Chapter 3). Cisgenderism refers to an ideology that views cisgender people (i.e. people whose gender identity matches the sex they were assigned at birth) as 'normal' and this has the effect of questioning everybody else's own designations of their gender (Ansara & Hegarty, 2013). As Riggs and Bartholomaeus (2020) show, due to 'compulsory cisgenderism', transgender people's experiences are routinely pathologised and 'Othered'. This can lead to a number of outcomes, that are both hostile and intended to belittle or shame, such as:

- **Misgendering:** When people use gendered descriptors that do not align with the pronouns that someone prefers to self-define or self-describe – such as calling someone 'he' when they would prefer to be called 'she'; or 'they' in the case of non-binary.
- **Erasing:** An unwillingness to acknowledge or recognise the existence of people who have gender identities outside of the 'norm'.
- **Pathologising:** Implying that a particular gender identity is invalid, or even pathological or perverted.
- **Binarising:** Claiming that genders exist only as a man/woman binary.

In a study that demonstrates the pervasiveness of cisgenderism, Howell and Allen (2020) ran a qualitative interview study looking at the schooling experiences of twelve *fa'afāfine* and *fakaleiti* in Aotearoa/New Zealand. Fa'afāfine is a Samoan word that translates as 'in the manner of' or 'like a woman', while fakaleiti is the Tongan equivalent (Schmidt, 2016). Fa'afāfine/fakaleiti are people who are assigned male gender at birth but perform their gender in a female manner. In their study, Howell and Allen interviewed fa'afāfine and fakaleiti people who attended an all-boys school. They belonged to a school peer support group known as 'The Goddesses', which provided support and mentors for those who identified as fa'afāfine or fakaleiti. All of the participants described experiences of bullying, verbal abuse, and pressure to conform to gender-specific 'displays', such as through their uniform choice. For example, Howell and Allen describe how rituals at the school were inherently cisgenderist: 'Each day, when teachers said, "Good morning boys", fa'afāfine and fakaleiti participants were misgendered and their identities erased' (Howell & Allen, 2020).

Challenging compulsory cisgenderism: The Trans Pregnancy Project

The Trans Pregnancy Project is a neat example of feminist scholarship that does not succumb to the compulsory cisgenderism of dominant discourses. The project addresses the sociological and health care implications of the reproductive practices of transgender and non-binary people who become pregnant and/or give birth after transitioning. The project has produced policy reviews that led to the creation of evidence-based best practice guides for staff working with transgender people navigating pregnancy.

The recent UK policy review (Trans Pregnancy Policy Review 7, United Kingdom), for example, explains how legislation such as the Human Fertilisation and Embryology Act 2008 is *cis-normative* and assumes that 'the individuals in question will have the reproductive capacities of cis males/females'.

SECTION SUMMARY

- A core element of a feminist approach to social psychology is a concern for equality, inclusion, and a preparedness to challenge dominant discourses to advocate for marginalised groups. Feminist social psychologists have therefore contributed a lot to the relationships literature over the years.
- Feminist contributions to the study of romantic relationships have primarily challenged heteronormativity (i.e. dominance of heterosexuality as 'the norm') and compulsory cisgenderism (i.e. dominance of being cisgender as 'the norm'), instead of championing more inclusive approaches to the study of relationships.

Rethinking evolutionary explanations

There is an area of psychological scholarship – evolutionary psychology – that tends to operate almost in isolation. It claims that it is evolution that has mainly shaped how human relationships are formed and performed, how we choose a lover, and how gender impacts on these processes. Its basic premise is that, when searching for a 'mate', women are attracted to resources – to men who are industrious (Langhorne & Secord 1955), physically attractive (Gangestad &

Buss, 1993), and rich! Townsend and Wasserman (1998) describe an 'universal tendency' for women to rely on men for substance and resources. Men, by contrast, are attracted by youth, feminine allure, and fertility. Sex and relationships are, by this account, highly pragmatic, as we humans have adopted hard-wired 'sexual selection strategies' over time, which serve to maximise men and women's chances of being sexually and reproductively successful.

Guess what? The vast majority of feminist social psychologists angrily dispute claims like these, dismissing evolutionary explanations of human relationships as nothing more than thought experiments, that (like neurosexism) tell very convincing stories but provide little evidence to back them up (Fausto-Sterling, 2000). Feminists have also taken issue with the ways in which 'mating behaviour' studies are overly concerned with masculine ideals, and fail to take women's mating choices seriously. Antoinette Brown Blackwell long ago summarised this nicely, stating that in Darwin's theory, 'the masculine force always predominates' (1875, p. 333). In other words – men are only happy when they are in charge.

Attractiveness

In the minority world, people are usually immersed in a social world that values aesthetics and beauty very highly. Our social media are continually shifting to include more image-based forms of communications (I'm looking at you, Instagram, and TikTok) and online dating is also highly visual. As the boom of Tinder in the 2010s demonstrated, we (think we) can tell a lot about a person by their looks. Understanding how people judge 'attractiveness' has been on the social psychology agenda for decades. However, if feminist social psychology teaches us anything, it's that human beings are usually more nuanced, subjective, and 'messy' than we would like to admit. Therefore, it perhaps does not come as a surprise that the vast majority of 'attractiveness' research conducted by mainstream social psychologists leaves much to be desired.

According to the mainstream social psychology literature, particularly in the social evolutionary field, we have a number of 'go to' markers of attractiveness that we use to decipher a person's good looks. So, sister feminists, in order to give you a beginner's guide for *How to Be Attractive to Men* (as informed by real social psychology research), we present to you the ultimate cheat sheet!

How To Be Attractive To Men (as evidenced by social psychology)

1 **Wear red:** Research demonstrates that there is a 'red-sex' link – women who wear red are judged to be more attractive. According to Elliot and Pazda (2012), the preference for red supposedly reflects a 'functional human universal', due to the 'societal conditioning' which associates the colour red with 'sex, romance, cosmetics, and prostitution' (although we prefer the term 'sex work'; see Bindman and Doezema, 1997).

2 **Have an hourglass figure:** In their *Social Psychology* textbook, Hogg and Vaughan (2018, p. 558) explain that 'typically, men prefer the classic hour-glass figure' due to the 'good genes hypothesis', which

claims that attractiveness is primarily determined by how young, fertile, and healthy women are perceived to be. Again, a high waist-to-hip ratio has been thought to be a 'universal' in terms of attractiveness, because it demonstrates to men women's 'reproductive potential', to use Singh's (2006) eloquent terminology.

3 **Ovulate:** In a review by Gangestad and Simpson (2000), a woman's fertility, or peak point within a menstrual cycle, is associated with perceived attractiveness. According to social evolutionary theory, when women are ovulating they prefer competitive, financially sound men, and men are most attracted to women during this time too. As Elliot and Pazda (2012) explain: 'when nearing ovulation, women are more easily sexually aroused, their general skin tone lightens, and they wear more revealing clothing'. The insidious transphobia of this idea is also not lost on us!

4 **Look young:** As evolutionary social psychologists teach, men prefer youthful-looking women, and women prefer rich-looking men. Young women tend to be more fertile women, which means that men are evolutionarily adapted to associate youth with reproductive fitness. It's a universal fact, ladies!

Of course, we are saying all this with tongue very much in cheek. These kinds of conclusions about 'universal' parameters of attractiveness are directly at odds with a feminist way of thinking. Findings like this are used to imply that 'universal attractiveness' operates in our life-world; inflexible blueprints of beauty for women and handsomeness for men that are encoded in our genes. 'There's nothing to be done about it' the evolutionists cry, 'it's in our very nature'.

The problematic nature of the evolutionary approach is, we hope, pretty clear. As a minimum, these clever stories of attractiveness simply don't account for the wide global diversity of what people find 'a turn on' and the ever-changing trends in style and perceptions of beauty. For example, Sypeck et al. (2006) have identified a change in perceived ideal BMI in females from 1979 to 1999 *Playboy* magazines (a publication seen as a barometer for sexual beauty ideals).

ACTIVITY 8.1: Biting back!

Now, as we did in Chapter 1, we're going to flip the script. Take each of the four 'attractiveness pointers' as set out above and rewrite them to fit your newly developing feminist perceptive apparatus. The ability to articulate our frustrations is an important piece of armour in our feminist toolkit; for example, Lewis (1990) notes that the articulation of perceptions, frustration, and anger can have 'transformative power' in establishing a feminist perspective. Take each of the four points and expose them to your crusading feminist battle-axe. Enjoy!

You may like to ask yourself:

- What *specifically* is problematic about these signposts of 'universal attractiveness'?
- How do they let us down as feminists?
- What might a feminist 'take' on these rules look like?

For example, to the first item ('Wear red! Men love it'), your 'feminist rewrite' may stress how women can, in fact, wear whatever colour they like. Wear red by all means, but for your own reasons – because it makes you happy, or to avoid the invisibility experienced in old age (bright red glasses are particularly effective). Alternatively, you might argue that women's value is not located in (a) judgements about their physical appearance, or (b) their ability to 'snare a mate'. You may have considered how 'the rules' ignore or devalue non-heterosexual forms of relationships. It also does not account for much diversity in preference or perception, and thus could be promoting a compulsory cisgender agenda. Finally, the idea that women should take any notice of these kinds of 'evolutionary rules' reinforces the 'man's world' discourse of **hegemonic masculinity**.

A note on fatphobia

For women, to be 'fat' is to fail at being a contemporary woman.
                              – Meredith Nash, *Making 'Postmodern' Mothers* (2012, p. 41)

In all cultures and societies, there are certain socially constructed mandates that women must live up to, in order to be 'adequately' feminine. For example, in the minority world there tends to be a powerful social mandate that women should be slender and conform to the social template of a beautiful, fertile, slim woman. As Grogan summarises so well, 'slenderness symbolises being in control' (2016, p. 11). Conversely, being overweight is associated with being 'out of control'. Clean-eating, therefore, is a matter of control, power, and self-management. In this sense, it also may lead to fat-shaming – that is, 'discrimination against fat people' (Kasardo & McHugh, 2015, p. 184). Cultural shifts have enforced self-schemas of eating that are difficult to break. This 'idealised thinness' reflects the idea that those who deviate from this cultural norm are in some way lacking, in both health and happiness (Chrisler, 2012).

A feminist reappraisal of sexual selection theory

According to evolutionary psychology, a woman's entire worth is her capacity for child-bearing. Indeed, it views females wholly and solely in relation to men. Not only does evolutionary theory dismiss recreational sex as merely a 'strategy experimentation' (Buss, 2016, p. 187), but the purpose of female orgasms is viewed as promoting men's success at impregnation – nothing is mentioned about their significance to, or meaning for, women.

Infantilisation and sexualisation

While we have been 'fooling around' somewhat throughout this chapter, the preference for women to look (and act) young and fertile has an impact in 'real-world' life. An example is the way it *infantilises* women. In 2010, for example, CNN politics reported that Elise Stefanik, a 33-year-old congresswoman from New York, was called a 'little girl', who 'can always run home to Mommy and Daddy', by her opponent in the debate. He later referred to her as 'sweetie' and 'a child'. Increasingly, thank goodness, this kind of behaviour is becoming unacceptable. About time too!

Evolutionary psychology dictates that women are attractive when they look young, fertile, and innocent. It draws a blurry line between the infantilisation of women and the sexualisation of youthful femininity. This fuels the 'sexy schoolgirls' trope that so often features in 'lads mags' and porn. This trope is dangerous as in sexualising girls it makes them vulnerable. E.J. Renold has done extensive research on the sexualisation of children in school (Renold, 2005) and discusses concepts of sexualisation of school uniform in great detail. For some female pupils, a school uniform is 'safer', as it detracts from 'girlie' femininities (like 'mini-skirts) to impress the boys. Even from elementary or primary-school age, modes of dress and outward appearance have become a standard way for children to express their gendered values. Together with Jessica Ringrose, Renold has turned to activism. They have chaired the Welsh Government's expert panel on the Healthy Relationships Curriculum in Wales, and they have developed resources to support feminist-informed teaching and learning about sexuality, including strategies to resist pressures on girls to become sexualised.

The sexualisation of young girls can become a toxic problem. One example of this, and a topic very close to my own heart (M.P.), is the banning of school skirts in UK high schools in an effort to 'protect young girls' from the *male gaze* and save male teachers' blushes. For example, in 2015, the headmistress of a high school in Stoke-on-Trent stated the rationale for banning school skirts was that short skirts were 'distracting male teachers' and the issue had becoming a 'safeguarding' concern. This directly forces the concept of overt femininity into the object of the – unwanted and unsolicited – male gaze. According to these rules, the sexualisation of school uniform could provoke young girls to view themselves as inevitable objects of the 'all-seeing' male gaze.

Feminist Darwinians

Certainly, there is no single way of 'doing' feminism in social psychology. While most feminists reject evolutionary psychology, there are, nonetheless, some compelling arguments from a few feminist scholars that evolutionary psychology has much to inform feminist psychology, and (importantly) vice versa. They challenge the notion that feminist and evolutionary approaches are wholly incompatible.

ACTIVITY 8.2: Adversarial collaboration

To think about this explicitly, locate the 2011 special issue of the journal *Sex Roles* that was edited by Christine Smith and Julie Konik. This special issue covers a whole host of nuanced considerations of how feminist psychologists and evolutionary psychologists may be allies, adversaries, or even both. In the journal, some psychologists use feminist theory to critique evolutionary psychology, as we have started to do here. However, other contributions call for an integration of feminist theory and evolutionary psychological ideas in an attempt to further our understanding of both areas. Griet Vandermassen (2011), for example, labels herself as a 'feminist Darwinian' and challenges the notion that feminist and evolutionary approaches are wholly incompatible.

The promise of 'adversarial collaborations'

Recall from Chapter 2 that social psychology is currently going through a 'replication crisis', which has suggested new ways of working and 'doing' psychological science in light of concerns about the robustness of social psychology's claims. In response to this, there is a whole host of innovative new tools to combat supposed biases in psychology research. One of these is '***adversarial collaborations***', whereby scholars from different – and typically conflicting – theoretical viewpoints run a study or project together which is designed to robustly test a research question. The idea is that scholars who have different ideas about what the results will look like work together to openly and transparently test their ideas together. They 'lay their cards on the table' and accept the outcome of the study, regardless of their ideological standpoint.

Given the critical suspicion or 'distrust' that exists between most evolutionary psychologists and most feminist psychologist (Eagly & Wood, 2011, p. 758), this may be fertile ground for some (rather interesting!) adversarial collaborations. Nier and Campbell's (2013) vision for a feminist future is collaboration between feminist and evolutionary psychologists, in attempts to resolve disagreements by coming to a consensus in the interpretation of data. This is a relatively high-risk research structure and requires a 'shared understanding' of research ***epistemology*** and methodology, which may be challenging to establish. However, adversarial collaborations are most definitely the future – you heard it here first!

SECTION SUMMARY

- We've now covered some thorny issues such as objectification, fatphobia, feminist evolutionary psychology, sexualisation, and attractiveness. We have also attempted to show you how feminist social psychologists can work to 'flip the script' on some of the more problematic areas of psychology, in a way that champions the values of feminism that we out-lined in Chapter 1.

- Importantly, we have also noted how not all feminists are alike! There is nearly as much debate and discussion happening within feminist social psychology as there is in psychology generally. Some feminists, for exam-ple, advocate for the study of evolutionary mechanisms and do not view feminism and evolution as incompatible, whereas others most definitely do. This is important because it demonstrates how much nuance there is in the study of feminist social psychology. There is more than one way of 'doing' feminism and one aim of this Companion is about getting you to consider what your way of 'doing' may be! – more on this in Chapter 9.

Female friendship

Female friendship gives depth and spirit to a political vision of feminism and is itself a profoundly political act. Without affection, our politics and political struggles remain superficial and more easily short-circuited. (Raymond, 2001, p. 29)

We now move on from talking about the study of *romantic* relationships to fem-inist work on the value of female friendship, given how closely this relationship has been studied and theorised by feminist scholars. There are profound gen-dered dynamics at play in female friendships, and it is often the space where women are able to 'break free' (albeit temporarily) from the impositions of *sex-ism* and gender norms. The nice thing about a feminist understanding of female friendships is that there are all kinds of representations in film, media, and music for you to peruse as you consider this relationship through a feminist lens. For example, in *Sex and the City* (a show that, we think, has much to teach us about feminist social psychology), after several series full of failed relationships, one of the 'gal pals' famously pondered: 'Maybe we can be each other's soul mates. And then we can let men be just these great, nice guys to have fun with'. At the time, this was shockingly revolutionary. Dumping the 'searching for your male soul mate' narrative that dominated many women's lives, and instead seeking that solace among your female friends, destabilises one of *patriarchy's* most power-ful mechanisms. Indeed, separatist feminists eschew having relationships with men, and seek to exclude them from their lives.

Feminist social psychologists have investigated the nuances of many differ-ent kinds of friendships, identifying how each one serves unique feminist func-tions. For example, there is a lively body of literature on girls' friendships, including a wonderful special issue of *Feminism & Psychology* (Frith, 2004, Volume 14, Issue 3). As you might expect, the study of friendships encompasses all kinds of political, societal, and psychological factors, and feminist social psychologists have taken to studying these with creativity and criticality.

The power of friendship has been a hallmark of feminist scholarship, most notably because of how well female friendship fits within the ideology of 'sisterhood' that has been a staple of the feminist movement (Rose & Roades, 1987). Therefore, as Martinussen et al. (2020) suggest, female friendships have 'radical potential', in that they make coping with the impact of *neoliberal* and *post-feminist* forces possible. For example, Martinussen et al. show how women's friendship can be a means of 'escaping the regimes of productivity' (2019, p. 8) by offering a comforting space away from the mandate of having to be 'nice'. In 1993, Miriam Zukas interviewed twenty women from a range of backgrounds about their female friendships. The women shared stories of changing and shifting friendship 'practices', which were determined by structural factors, including class, gender, and race.

However, despite the possibility that female friendships can be closely aligned to a feminist agenda, some feminist psychologists have urged us to reconsider who this may be silencing or marginalising. For example, in 1992, Wilton published a gloriously personal and political essay in *Feminism & Psychology*, which suggested that viewing female friendships is equivalent to feminism rendering lesbianism 'invisible', much as patriarchy has always done (1992, p. 507). Wilton also notes that heteronormativity and patriarchy are institutions, and female friendships primarily exist *within* them. Therefore, assuming that 'close female friendships' can get entangled with the 'sisterhood' of feminism can serve to trivialise the salience of lesbian romantic relationships.

The role of female friendships is often *intersectional*, i.e. friendships look different and serve different purposes depending on the identities that intersect. For example, *global majority* women's friendship may well be markedly different from the friendship between minority women where the stereotypes and gender norms placed on these groups of women are different. For example, American women of colour may face stereotyping related to sexuality and motherhood that serves to further marginalise them (Collins, 2000). Experiences of multiple marginalisation can shape the ways that friendships can operate. For example, Goins (2011) described how female friendships represent 'a homeplace of safe space' for Black women, offering a space for *empowerment* and resistance with which to counter intersectional oppression.

Feminist psychology and motherhood

Given that feminist social psychology is keen to (re)capture and (re)claim the experiences of girls and women in mainstream spaces, it is perhaps not surprising that 'motherhood' is an important space for feminist analysis. From a social psychology perspective, the experiences of *becoming* and *being* a mother are woven into all kinds of social phenomena (such as social identities) and social practices (such as 'doing daughter' and 'doing grandma'). For example, in her classic text, Bailey (1999) discussed the 'refraction' of self-identity during the transition to motherhood, taking particularly note of women's attempts to maintain a coherent sense of self during pregnancy and early motherhood, specifically in relation to their gendered and embodied identity. Throughout pregnancy, women must create, or envision, a new maternal self. Women have reported feeling a loss of autonomy and loss of their pre-pregnancy self (Barclay et al., 1997). Feminist research has also observed how the biological transition to becoming a mother is sometimes associated with women's feelings about their own body pre- and postpartum, which Upton and Han (2003) describe as a loss of 'body self'. Indeed, throughout pregnancy, women may go through a process of 'recapturing, redefining, and reclaiming' their body (Ogle et al., 2011, p. 35).

The motherhood mandate

Feminist social psychologists see, within minority world societies, a tendency to position motherhood as central to the characterisation of womanhood (Russo, 1976). Women are 'propelled' into motherhood through the proliferation of sex stereotypes, gender norms, and societal pressures. This means that childfree women, particularly those who work full time, can be treated as having a damaged identity (see Chapter 3). For example, research shows that childfree women are perceived to be incomplete, inauthentic, or abnormal, overly career-oriented (or 'workaholics') and 'free riders' who don't participate in a 'collective duty' of childrearing (Abma & Martinez, 2006; Verniers, 2020). While the vast majority of women do become mothers, recent statistics in the minority world tend to show an increase in the number of childfree women. For example, in the United States, 26.2% of women aged 30–34 years were childfree in 2006, but by 2016 that had risen to 30.8% (United States Census Bureau, 2017). However, mainstream social psychology research typically neglects these kind of trends and largely adopts a 'one-size-fits-all' approach.

This idea that motherhood is a critical aspect of womanhood has been discussed by feminists for decades. In her landmark book *The Feminine Mystique* (1963), Betty Friedan wrote compellingly about 'the problem that has no name', which was the problem arising from the way in which, in those times in the USA and beyond, women were expected to willingly accept the role of wives – and especially mothers – as their *natural* destiny. This is the crux of the 'motherhood mandate'. As Turnbull et al. explain, the motherhood mandate is prompted by 'ideologies, discourses and policies that construct motherhood as natural and central to being a woman, and impose a moral, patriotic and economic obligation on women to procreate' (2017, p. 334).

Constructions of 'good mothering'

Beyond the stigma associated with electing *not* to have children, there is additional stigmatisation associated with *how* women go about mothering. Susan Douglas and Meredith Michaels (2005), for example, demonstrate how the pressure to be 'the perfect mother' has intensified over time. The identity of 'the doting, self-sacrificing mother' has become the ideal to which all mothers should aspire. Sharon Hays' *The Cultural Contradictions of Motherhood* (1996) begins by recognising the immense pressure involved when being positioned as a mother with all manner of expectations about making sacrifices and so on, and yet, she notes, there is little recognition of the 'circumstances, power relations and interests' involved in laying this obligation on women (1996, p. 156).

This 'good mothering' mandate is largely fuelled by prominent discourses about what 'good mothering' looks like, which Miller (2007) notes is informed by 'old wives' tales', maternal experiences, and conventional stereotypes. Although these are socially constructed discourses (i.e. the idea of what constitutes 'good mothering' reflects cultural and social norms), they are readily perceived to be 'true' and thus serve as 'the standard' for modern mothering (Blum & Stracuzzi, 2004). This notion of one 'good mothering' blueprint is in direct contradiction with the decades of feminist research which shows how diverse the experiences of birth, childrearing, and mothering can be.

The iconic image of perfect motherhood has a cost for women – feelings of guilt, in particular, at failing to attain the ideal; of shame, inadequacy, and frustration – not to mention simple exhaustion! Johnston and Swanson (2007) use the term 'cognitive acrobatics' to describe the way that mothers have to constantly juggle their other commitments alongside their aspirations to be a 'good mother' – this they found to be true whether women were working or not. Henderson and her colleagues conclude that 'the ideology of being the 'perfect mother' is inescapable; it is far-reaching and negatively affects mothers who do not even buy into it' (Henderson, Harmon, & Newman, 2016, p. 514). It becomes, they say, an 'inescapable cultural mandate'. Concern about mothering is recognised to be strongly intersectional, where the ideal of 'mother' is held to be highly normative – heterosexual, able-bodied, middle class, and of an appropriate age. Mothers falling outside of this ideal can be frowned upon, especially in the way they can be treated by service providers, such as some health visitors and social workers.

See and hear for yourself

There are numerous films and television programmes that shine some feminist light on the intricacies of both motherhood and friendship. The 2017 movie 'Lady Bird' is a personal favourite of mine (M.P.). This 'coming of age' film tells the story of a teenage girl's slightly bumpy, if not loving relationship with her mother and friends. As you watch this, look in particular at how Lady Bird's mother is constructed on screen.

SECTION SUMMARY

Examining both female friendships and mothering allows us to critically consider how women's relationships are constructed by society in particularly stereotyping ways. There is a large and powerful body of literature which identifies the nuances of motherhood from a feminist perspective, calling into question issues such as the 'motherhood mandate', constructions of 'good mothering', and the social identity negotiations involved in becoming a mother.

A note on reflexivity

In the second half of this chapter, we have focused primarily on the nature of female friendship and the role of 'being a mother' As feminist social psychologists, when we study these kinds of 'real-world' roles and relationships, it is useful to reconsider the issue of **reflexivity** that we first introduced you to in Chapter 2. As you move on in your journey as a feminist social psychologist, consider how the critical feminist theories, ideas, and debates that you read in this Companion can inform your own *reflexive practice*. For example, you may wish to spend some time reflecting on your own constructions of motherhood, and how they may be limited. Consider where your assumptions come from and what you may need to do to expand your insight and understanding.

CHAPTER SUMMARY

- In this chapter, we have been rather sceptical over the claims of social evolutionary psychology about the nature of romantic relationships, what constitutes attractiveness, and 'mating behaviour'.
- We have learnt about the ways in which evolutionary ideas typically position women as passive and men as active, but have also considered the nuances of feminist ideas about the tension between evolutionary and feminist ideas.
- We have used female friendships and motherhood as two examples of roles and relationships that provide a useful appraisal of feminist advocacy for the experiences of girls and women at play.

Looking forward to your fabulous feminist future

Phew – we're nearly there! The journey into (and through) feminist social psychology can sometimes be a bit of a bumpy ride, and sometimes more like an exciting roller-coaster. But we do hope it hasn't been boring. So far in this Companion, we have done our best to get across what feminism offers you as a social psychologist – and, we hope, a budding feminist. This last chapter is a little different. Here, we are mainly concerned with looking to the future and we hope our book will have set you on an interesting trek, building on what you have learned and inspiring you to go further.

Expanding your feminist consciousness

In this Companion, we have only been able to touch on a small part of a large (and rapidly expanding) bounty of feminist scholarship and activism in social psychology. Coming to the end of the book, we will explore how you could (if you so wish) develop your *feminist consciousness* – where being a feminist becomes part of who you are and how you see the world. We want to get you thinking about how *you* can contribute to tackling the feminist agendas we've identified throughout this book – such as engaging in public education (formal and informal) about the troubles that women have suffered; providing services tailored to women's needs and entitlements – such as safe abortions within non-judgemental and emancipatory settings; and actions taken to resist the sexualisation of young girls and sexual harassment in the classroom. Here, we will present you with a smorgasbord of various nuggets of feminist activism. Some are highly creative, some are great fun, some are very serious, and most involve an awful lot of very hard work; but all are wonderful examples of feminist social psychology well and truly 'in action'.

Citation as 'conscientious engagement'

Developing a feminist consciousness needs to become an everyday routine. A good start is to get into a mindset where you are always very thoughtful about how you cite the work of others. Mott and Cockayne (2017) have written a really helpful paper, albeit about geography rather than psychology, but they are challenging the dominance of what they call a 'white heteromasculinism'. In it, they set out the key issues involved and give pointers to how citation can be made a practice of 'conscientious engagement' – one that avoids perpetuating academic misogyny and colonialism. Citation, they argue, 'is important because the choices we make about whom to cite – and who is left out of the conversation' (2017, p. 955) matter. Geography, they argue, is 'unduly informed by experiences of whiteness' (p. 959). So, too, is psychology. Both need us to ask some fundamental questions about our citation praxis:

- How is knowledge reproduced and remembered here?
- How are its histories narrated, and by whom?
- How are today's neoliberal academic environments moulding and shaping who gets cited and who does not?

ACTIVITY 9.1: Take up the fight with us

If you search the term 'Feminist activism in … (choose a country or community)', you are likely to find evidence that *something* is certainly going on. I tried it with Ghana, as a couple of years ago I listened to a brilliant paper given by a Ghanaian health psychologist and she really made an impression on me, so I thought it would be fertile ground. It certainly was, and I learned a great deal.

Do something like this yourself with a place from where you have never seen anything cited in an academic journal before. Then spend at least thirty minutes getting the best handle you can on the feminist activism going on there. Reflect upon your experiences doing this activity and think what people like you could do to make this knowledge better known among your own community. Doing this as a group activity would be a perfect way to spread the word. What have you learned? What could you do next?

Calling out everyday sexism

This works by acquiring a kind of radar; that is, heightening your sensitivity to the subtle indications that you are being treated in a ***sexist*** (or otherwise hostile) manner – being subtly put down, diminished, or ***gaslighted***. Even without any knowledge about feminism, many women get a 'gut feeling' that what is going on is a bit dodgy. If it goes unrecognised, everyday sexism like this can seriously undermine people and destroy their confidence to speak. Reading Laura Bates's book, *Everyday Sexism* (2016), is an excellent way to start exploring the relentless barrage of tiny but persistent jibes and the kind of subtle hectoring-lecturing that constitute everyday sexism.

Recognising ***mansplaining*** all started with Rebecca Solnit, who wrote a powerful essay titled *Men Explain Things to Me* (2014). There are three people in Solnit's story – herself, her female friend, and a man who joined them uninvited. He was terribly keen to tell them about a brilliant new book that he had found out about. Throughout the conversation, he does his best to silence her friend's attempts to interrupt him (to tell him that it was Solnit who wrote the book he was talking about). Clearly, it had not crossed his mind that she could possibly be the author! Solnit's view is that mansplaining 'is not a universal flaw of the gender, more the intersection between overconfidence and cluelessness' (2014, para. 3).

In terms of developing this aspect of feminist consciousness, we have been inspired by a recent paper written by a fabulous group of feminists – Jack Joyce, Bogdana Huma, Hanna-Leena Ristimäki, Fabio Ferraz de Almeida, and Ann Dohring. In it they have deployed discursive and conversational analyses to root out and expose how mansplaining operates (Joyce et al., 2021, p. 1). As a consequence of research like this, new vocabularies have been invented that make it possible for feminists to draw attention to sexism and misogyny when they meet it. Words like mansplaining, alongside **bropriating, sealioning**, and **manterrupting**, give feminists a language to highlight what is going on. Words like these are powerful because they make bad behaviour talk-about-able. Getting familiar with them and using them when you spot the action will mean you will no longer collude with misbehaviour being 'swept under the carpet' and hidden from view.

It takes a certain amount of courage to call out sexism like this. We can hope that as challenges to misbehaviour become more common, we can become more effective. It is part of what Sarah Ahmed calls 'becoming a **feminist killjoy**' (Ahmed, 2016; also see her blog). Predominantly, this is about being willing to systematically complain about misbehaviour and, indeed, about when people fail to act when wrongs are being done. We are ourselves somewhat ambivalent about reinforcing the image of feminists as sour, bitter, and dry old creatures always 'whingeing on'. We prefer the gutsy and spirited version of women who come across as justifiably angry and frustrated and who refuse to go along with the pejorative language that patriarchy reserves for women who rock the boat (there is a lot on this in Chapter 7). They reject the way they get called 'wilful' and 'stubborn', 'harping' and 'nagging' when men behaving in the same way are depicted as powerful, brave, and masterful – and they say so in no uncertain fashion. But sometimes the odd complaint is simply the only way to get heard.

So, how to challenge them?

If you think back to Chapter 1, you will recall the way that Carol Tavris countered claims that women are wimps, inadequate, and in the wrong, by reversing the depictions:

> Women are not 'gullible'; men are inflexible. Women are not 'humourless'; men do not know what is funny. (Tavris, 1993, p. 151)

She sets a great example – and we, too, can contest sexism with a kind of wry smile, but nonetheless making a point. Here's some examples:

Him:	Well, that's all a matter of common sense – women are naturally …
You:	How d'you know it's natural? What's your evidence?
Man:	You shouldn't be fussing yourself about all that in your state.
Woman:	I've had a baby, not a lobotomy.

Building your feminist toolkit

If you decide you want to take on the role of 'Fabulous Feminist' in the place where you study or work, then you need to gather some resources around you. First, you will need some allies, so do seek out others who may already be taking this role. You should already have quite a lot to build on, following your work in Chapter 4.

Activity	Resource	Action
4.1	Information about the history of feminism where you are	Find out how this can be a resource where you are working or studying and make it so
4.2	List of barriers women face to full participation	Make a plan of action to make the necessary changes
4.3	Information about what constitutes 'domestic abuse', 'domestic violence', and 'intimate violence' in the legal jurisdiction where you live/work	Compile a collection of documents or files dealing with each of these. Or you could create a webpage. Build them into a resource that will be useful to anyone experiencing these forms of violence
	Statistical information about the rates of domestic violence where you are – differences between male and female perpetrators, taking the severity into account	
	Your thoughts about the impact upon the victims, children in the household, women in general, and men in general	
4.4	A series of documents/sources setting out the rights of people you study/work with, in terms of the law, the code of conduct where you study/work, and what procedures are in place to make complaints	Create databases with all this information on it and make it accessible. Check out what is already there and find out if/how you can add to it. Draw in particular on what has been achieved and look for people to work with you
	Documents, web-links, and contact details of support services available to offer advice and support for making complaints about types of mistreatment, including informal ones	
7.1	Your expanded knowledge about the language strategies that men can use to deny their own agency, and hence responsibility for misbehaviour	Develop your capacity to recognise when this is going on, and your courage to call it out

Feminist activism

There is a whole body of social psychology literature that critically discusses how feminist activism has come to be, what it looks like, and how people 'end up' becoming activists. This includes studies that explore how feminist identity is linked to activism pursuits (Yoder, Tobias, & Snell, 2011), predictors of change in activism (Stake, 2007), and commentaries on instances of feminist activism, such as the Women's March (Martin & Smith, 2020). There are also useful profiles that celebrate the lives and contributions of 'lifelong feminist activists'. For example, a useful 2014 paper by Anjali Dutt and Shelly Grabe subtitled 'Narratives of lifelong feminist activists committed to social change', analysed the oral histories of prominent 'lifelong feminists' using an idiographic methodology, which centres on the experiences of three notable feminists. Dutt and Grabe (2014) tell the story of Matilde Lindo, who was a Black feminist and leader of the Autonomous Women's Movement in Nicaragua. Lindo was particularly interested in exposing and challenging violence against women and worked with many different activist-oriented organisations. She later went on to join the Women's Network Against Violence. The paper also provides an idiographic account of the life and work of Daud Sharifa Khanam, a feminist activist who was known for helping to build the first Mosque in India that was exclusively for women. This was linked to her work in establishing the first network of Muslim women in southern India, the 'Tamil Nadu Muslim Women's Jamaat' Committee.

Inspiring your activism

At this point, we want to share four stories of feminist activism in action as described by the activists themselves. Again, this is only a sliver of the massive body of scholarship and activism that feminist social psychologists have built over the years, but it's a good place to begin. You will notice that some of these are very psychology-centric, whereas others show how feminist social psychologists can use their expertise to work with multidisciplinary teams of feminists in action. Importantly, they are all tied to some of the core concerns that we have raised throughout this Companion, including (but by no means limited to) concerns about gender inequality, motherhood discrimination, gender bias, and *social justice*.

Case Study 1: Feminist-focused abortion counselling training

Yamini Kalyanaraman, Jabulile Mary-Jane Jace Mavuso, Ryan du Toit, and Catriona Ida Macleod, Rhodes University, University of Pretoria, and University of KwaZulu-Natal, South Africa

'The scary thing is the counselling can make us run away'. These are the words of Zimkhitha, a woman we interviewed at an abortion clinic in South Africa as part of a study on women's experiences of abortion counselling. We also recorded actual counselling sessions. These revealed high levels of directive counselling essentially designed to do what Zimkhitha indicated – make abortion seekers run away. Abortion was often depicted as awful – leading to severe psychological and physical outcomes, even death ('there's of course termination which is risky to your body. You can see in the consent form it says you can die'). Personhood was ascribed to the foetus ('The baby is already this size. This is a little model, just to show you exactly the size of your baby') to morally delegitimise abortion *and* to enforce motherhood as a sacred duty ('when God puts that baby in your stomach, he also puts it in your heart').

This research was conducted through the Critical Studies in Sexualities and Reproduction research unit, located at Rhodes University in Makhanda, South Africa. The overarching goal of the research programme is to conduct critical research that addresses the social dynamics undermining full sexual and reproductive citizenship for all. To do so, we adopt a post-colonialist, post-structuralist feminist engaged research approach.

In the spirit of engaged research, we used these findings to develop a policy brief, a step-by-step guide to non-directive women-centred counselling, and an abortion counselling training course for in-service nurses. We formed a partnership with the Eastern Cape Department of Health, and obtained accreditation from Rhodes University to run the online training course. At the same time, we commenced an action research project, using the cycle of planning, implementing, observing, reflecting, and re-implementing to improve the course. Participants who completed the course indicated, among other things, that: they understood the importance of advocating for their clients; they had acquired self-respect as providers despite significant stigma, as well as respect for their clients; and they formed a peer support group, especially when presented with difficult cases.

Case Study 2: Stitching stories of survival and resistance

Puleng Segalo, Professor of Psychology, University of South Africa

Colonialism and later apartheid in South Africa rendered women (Black women in particular) as second-class citizens. Denied a voice and exposed to perpetual violence both in their private spaces and in public, many women had to find ways to survive state violence in public, and intimate partner violence in their private spaces. In the post-apartheid South Africa, many women continue to embody scars of the past and are haunted by unspeakable traumas they experienced while growing up in an oppressive world. I am interested in the ways in which women reflect and make meaning of their lived experiences – that is, growing up during apartheid South Africa and then living in a democratised country. What strategies do women use to express how they navigated growing up in an oppressive patriarchal government system? I found that speaking about their life (about suffering, displacement, loss, pain, etc.) was insufficient, and therefore, exploring other ways to express 'the unspeakable' lived experiences was necessary.

This is where visual methodologies became useful. Working collaboratively with a group of community women, we used embroideries to visually carve stories of Black women who survived apartheid. The embroideries offered layers of their lives and visually depicted narratives of survival, resistance, pain, loss, and hope. The embroideries have become moving monuments of women's life histories. The work was exhibited for six months at the Venice biennale in 2019 as part of the Auschwitz Institute for Peace and Reconciliation project to showcase the connections between art, human rights, and mass atrocity prevention. The work is currently at the Canadian Museum of Human Rights in Winnipeg, Canada, where the exhibition will be on permanent display from April 2021 until January 2022. Through this collaborative embroidery project, the women tell (travelling) stories of survival to show what is possible; to highlight that women are not helpless and voiceless victims of societal brutality – that they can contribute towards imagining the possibility of a peaceful and just world.

Case Study 3: Ruler HeART Activisms

E.J. Renold, Professor of Childhood Studies, Cardiff University, Wales

In the spring of 2015, together with a group of 15-year-old teen girls, we made a graffitied ruler-skirt to raise awareness of sexual harassment and violence, in school, online, and in their community – a post-industrial semi-rural Welsh valleys town (Libby et al., 2018). The girls took up our invitation to work with some of the anonymised data on gendered and sexual violence that surfaced in the interview transcripts during the first phase of a youth community research engagement project on safe and unsafe places (www.productivemargins.co.uk). Unplanned, the idea to create a ruler-skirt arose from a throw-away comment by one of the girls: 'Boys lift up girls' skirts with rulers'. It was one of those moments where an affective 'snap' (Ahmed, 2016) meets creative and speculative methodologies (Coleman et al., 2019) and 'things in the making cut their transformational teeth' (Massumi, 2015, p. ix).

As soon as the words were voiced into the space, another girl scribbled in bold black capital letters: 'RULER TOUCHING' and an explosion of ruler-talk erupted about how rulers are used to sexually assault (e.g. up-skirting) and shame girls (e.g. measuring skirt length), how experiences of sexual violence are often ruled out (e.g. normalised and silenced), and how gender norms are used to regulate who you can be and what you can do ('rule her, RULE HER, rule her with your ruler').

The girls began re-writing the rules and outing practices that sexually shame girls on printed paper rulers. These tuned into paper 'shame chains'. They then graffitied over thirty acrylic rulers with similar messages that hurt and abuse, but which were interspersed with messages for change (e.g. 'respect us'). As ideas about assembling the rulers to create a wearable piece of fashion activism were in full swing, the proposal for a ruler-skirt struck a chord. Each graffitied ruler was clipped to a belt, and the skirt began to take shape. What was once a phallic object that sexually assaults now swing-slaps as a more-than-human agent of change and has been stirring up a series of future ruler-risings ever since – which, in the words of the girls, are beginning to 'make our feelings matter'.

Informed by a post-qualitative, post-human, feminist, new materialist praxis (see www.phematerialisms.org), it has touched and been touched by policy-makers, politicians, civil servants, and members of the public and even visited the United Nations Headquarters in New York, swinging into action alongside the First Minister for Wales sharing the advances being made on Welsh policy to address gender equality and Relationships and Sexuality Education (RSE). The skirt kick-started the Valentine Card Youth Activism where over 1,000 children wrote on paper rulers why they wanted a better RSE and pasted them into valentine cards which were hand delivered to every politician in Wales. It also sparked the making of the arts-activist relationships and sexuality education AGENDA resource for children, young people, and practitioners (www.agendaonline.co.uk/ruler-heart), which has reached over 7,000 young people in the UK, in Wales, England, Ireland, New York, Australia, and Finland and is supporting teachers co-produce the RSE curriculum with their students (Renold, Ashton, & McGeeney, 2021).

Ruler-activisms have been making ripples and waves in and across policy, practice, and activist spaces ever since (Renold, 2019; Renold & Timperley, 2021). And when making youth voice matter on issues and experiences inevitably incites toxic media attention and personally targeted attacks, the research artefacts come into their own. They throw out a life-line and live on to affect, inspire, and inform a gender and sexuality youth justice to come.

Case Study 4: Participatory methods in maternal peri-natal mental health

Dr Tanya Beetham and Dr Siân Lucas, University of Stirling

While all women are at risk of developing peri-natal mental health issues, those who experience poverty, migration, extreme stress, violence, and lack social support are at greater risk of experiencing difficulties with their mental health. Recent policy and guidance in Scotland suggest that the needs of women experiencing mental health difficulties in the peri-natal period should be addressed, but there exists a gap between policy and practice, which our project aimed to address (World Health Organization, 2016). To do this, we wanted to centre the voices and experiences of women who access the service.

We worked with a family centre to establish a study advisory group of women who had accessed the peri-natal mental health service (Lucas & Beetham, 2019). The service was part of Quarriers, which is a Scottish charity that provides support and care for children, adults, and families throughout the UK. In 2001, the Ruchazie Family Centre was established in the north-east of Glasgow. The Family Centre provides early years care and family support delivered by a multidisciplinary team. In our research with this service, women worked with us to design the research, carry out some of the research, and analyse the data. We found that there is great value in participatory methods with voices that are usually marginalised, less heard, and less visible. Attending to relationships and a commitment to community-led research is vital. We suggest that a reflexive, community-oriented, and flexible approach is useful for other feminist researchers using participatory methods.

Activism more broadly

Reclaiming her-story

The Global Feminisms project situated at the University of Michigan demonstrates the power of collective action (Lal et al., 2010). The project centres around interviews with women's movement activists and women's studies scholars in sites around the world. By sharing these stories of feminist scholarship and activism in action, the project aims to 'bring understandings of activism, historical context, identity formation, and social movements into play'. This noble pursuit is similar to that of the Psychology's Feminist Voices archive, a resource that we have drawn on throughout this Companion, which centres the voices of prominent women scholars throughout psychology's past (and present!).

Polling for justice

Brett Stoudt, Madeline Fox, and Michelle Fine's (2012) collaborative research project 'Polling for Justice' is a great illustration of feminist social psychology that is very much 'in action'. The project aims to collectively explore notions and constructs of privilege together with young people and adults in New York City. This is a lovely example of activism-engaged research. For instance, in their discussion of the research project, the authors explain how they 'gathered together young and old with very different kinds of expertise, while honouring most significantly those who have lived lives under the thumb of structural injustice' (2012, p. 180). By taking this stance, the group openly seeks to counter the kinds of research that *blame* young people for social problems. Research like this can lead to beneficial changes in policy, social conditions, and cultural representations. This is a neat example of how the way that we approach research as social psychologists can have a real impact on bringing about policy change.

Challenging the motherhood penalty

In the previous chapter, we talked a bit about the challenges that mothers face in the workplace, and indeed beyond. In the UK, an activist group has been set up called 'Pregnant Then Screwed' (www.pregnantthenscrewed.com). It comprises lawyers, psychologists, activists, and volunteers all set on challenging the *motherhood penalty*. This group was set up by Joeli Brearley after she was sacked from her job when her employer learned that she was pregnant with her first child. Joeli explains that the group 'believe[s] in a world where women are not judged for the contents of their womb, or the hours they work, or the fact that they have porridge in their hair and smell of Sudocrem, but for their skills and talents'. There are other groups who concentrate on specific *intersections* of the motherhood penalty, for example, the group 'Black Mums Matter Too' provides free perinatal support to Black mums in the UK.

Running craftivist workshops

One of our favourite ways of attending critically to the idea of feminist social psychology 'in action' has been to attend craftivist workshops run by a growing number of feminists. In these workshops, women get together to combine doing familiar 'women's crafts' (such as embroidery, knitting, pottery) as a form of activism (such as consciousness-raising). Crafting together as a group of women (or, sometimes, more as a group of feminists) provides a comfortable and familiar setting within which women can talk together discretely (often without looking at each other) about intimate things. These also importantly 'reclaim' some of the assumptions of traditional femininity and turn the notion of 'women's work' well and truly on its head. You have already seen how E.J. Renold found running workshops a fantastic way to build feminist inventiveness and commitment to action, and how Puleng Segalo used wall-hanging embroidery to tell stories that are hard to tell. Here are two more examples:

Foof-felting

Herself a highly skilled needle-felter (her Christmas Robins are exquisite), Victoria Clarke has devised and run a series of Design-A-Vagina workshops where she teaches participants how to 'foof-felt' to create vivid and often rather beautiful representations of pudenda/vaginas. Some are pretty plain representations, but other women embellish their 'foofs' with beads and sometimes even pearl beads and glitter to make them eye-catching works of art. Clarke aims to 'empower vagina owners to talk comfortably and knowledgably about their genitals'. She notes that 'Crafting is a great tool for teaching about genital anatomy and diversity'. It's also a great way to celebrate female bodies as beautiful rather than shameful. This can be extended to all different kinds of bodies too – using craft to appreciate, honour, and celebrate the body is a powerful tool!

Beautifying or brutalising Barbie

A second example are the workshops run by Paula Singleton (2020) to get women (including young women in schools) to explore their image of what an authentic woman looks like and, in so doing, talk about their concerns about the expectations of 'femininity' promoted by popular culture. Singleton describes one of her first workshops in some detail. In it she handed out a Barbie doll to each participant plus a lot of craft materials like glue, card, felt-tip pens, glitter, plastic, and ribbons 'to have fun with'. When the girls got to work on their dolls, they were asked to make it better represent the way she saw her real self.

Singleton reports how one girl got there late, in a foul mood, having been 'up before the bench' (i.e. appeared before a criminal court). She was obviously very angry, and, having had none of the gentle warm-up with which the session began, she reacted immediately with much aggression, snatched the doll and started attacking it, besmirching its face, jabbing at its body, and cutting its hair to look awful. Singleton reflects extensively in her paper how the image of this doll continued to haunt her for a very long time. It 'hit a nerve' and made her think. The paper is well worth reading in full, as it describes in depth the extent to which work like this can generate very strong emotions and must be undertaken with care. For example, Singleton arranged for three familiar youth workers to take part in the workshop, who could offer support when needed. But she also notes how productive it can be.

Nurturing your networks and getting nurtured by them

Feminist social psychologists are a collaborative, friendly, communal bunch. We know we can do a whole lot more as a collective than we can ever achieve alone! As testament to this, there are a number of organisations, self-organised groups, and informal spaces where you can meet other likeminded feminist social psychologists. The groups here are predominantly based in either the UK or the US, but welcome participation from other countries. Just now we have a very lovely group of feminist psychologists from Iceland, and another group from Portugal who definitely keep us on our toes.

POWES: The Psychology of Women and Equalities Section (POWES) of the British Psychology Society is the hub of feminist psychology in the UK. We could even say it is the beating heart of feminist psychology. There is a Facebook discussion group, a publication (aptly named POWER), and a very popular annual conference. POWES aims to address gender issues and inequalities, facilitate and disseminate feminist research, and ultimately use this to inform policy.

Association of Women in Psychology (AWP): AWP (https://www.awpsych.org/) is an organisation that aims to address a myriad of concerns and issues that broadly sit at the intersection between feminism and psychology. In recent years, this has included speaking out against racism in psychology, publishing press releases urging activism for issues such as reproductive justice and sex education, and advocating for diversity.

Society for the Psychology of Women (Division 35 of APA): North America's equivalent to POWES (https://www.apadivisions.org/division-35)! Div. 35 (as it's commonly known) takes an intersectional approach to the psychology of women by focusing on communities centred around concerns and interests related to race, ethnicity, sexual orientation, and gender diversity. As an organisation it has unique 'Sections' which each attend to various intersections of feminism and psychology; for example, there is a 'Psychology of Black Women' section, and a 'Lesbian, Bisexual, and Transgender Concerns' section.

Society for the Psychological Study of Social Issues (SPSSI): SPSSI (https://www.spssi.org/) is an academic organisation but has a very firm hold on policy, legislation, and activism. SPSSI aims to connect psychological research on social issues, such as inequalities, racism, and gender-based violence, to public policy in a meaningful and informed way. It publishes policy briefings, works in partnership with legislators, and collates resources for teaching social justice issues in psychology. And it also has a wonderfully lively conference every year!

Gender and Education Association (http://www.genderandeducation. com) is a charity, a community of educators, researchers, activists, leaders, artists, working to challenge and eradicate gender stereotyping, sexism, and gender inequality within and through education.

Resources

The Women in Academia Support Network (WIASN): WIASN (https:// www.wiasn.com/) is a closed Facebook network that aims to recognise, challenge, and support women's experiences of navigating academia. This includes discussions offering peer support on emotional labour in academia, gendered prejudice and discrimination, and the continuous critical appraisal of women's intelligence at work.

Feminist Killjoys has been set up by Sara Ahmed as a resource to support feminist activism (https://feministkilljoys.com). In it you will find an archive of her blog-posts, which report and comment on all sorts of activism, especially around 'making complaints' as a means of bringing about change.

Rewriting the Rules is both a book and a website (https://www.rewriting-the-rules.com) created by Meg John Barker. It contains a blog and offers access to an incredible range of zines on subjects related to sexuality, gender, self-help, and so on. Meg John has a background in counselling psychology. They worked at the Open University but left academia to become an independent therapist, writer, presenter, discussant, and much else.

BME Psychology (https://bmepsychology.com) was set up and is maintained by Glen Jankowski, a psychology lecturer at Leeds Beckett University. This website houses a growing collection of resources for decolonising psychology.

Onwards and upwards

And that's a wrap! In this chapter, we have considered how we can apply all of the wonderful feminist perspectives on social psychology to the 'real world'. We have introduced you to ways that you can now take this on by engaging with feminist social psychology academically and getting involved in activism. Remember this doesn't have to be curtains! Look up some of the organisations and groups that we have introduced you to here and get involved – or consider setting up a craftivist workshop (with a little help from some feminist friends). Maybe we will even see you on the dance floor at a POWES Conference one day – do come and say hello if you do!

Glossary

In a world where an Internet search will find you the meaning of most words, we have made this Glossary highly selective. We have restricted ourselves to terms that:

- we have either invented or appropriated from others directly or modified somewhat; and
- those that have a particular meaning and/or history in the context of the feminist social psychology ideas and approaches in this Companion.

The terms included here are indicated in the text by being set *italic + bold* the first time they occur in each chapter. Mostly they are defined in some detail on first use, but the Glossary is intended to be useful where they pop up over again in later chapters. If you are a student, you may also find the definitions here useful in preparing your assignments.

Adversarial collaborations are a means whereby scholars from different – and, typically, conflicting – theoretical viewpoints run a study or project together which is designed to robustly test research questions. The idea is that scholars who have different ideas about what the results will look like work together to openly and transparently test their ideas together. They 'lay their cards on the table' and accept the outcome of the study, regardless of their ideological standpoint.

Androcentrism is a **worldview** that regards the male as the standard, from which females are judged as wanting, lacking, or second best. Women and girls are Othered rather than being seen as equally human alongside men. It is pernicious as it is so deeply woven into what people (both men and women) regard as 'common sense' or 'what everybody knows' – so much so that any challenge to it can be resisted by calling to reason – the way things are is fine, so why are you making trouble?

ANROWS (Australia's National Research Organisation for Women and Safety) is an excellent source of research into **sexism**.

Benevolent sexism is a subtle form of **sexism** which often looks like chivalry or gallantry. It can be used as a form of **gaslighting**, where a woman is constantly being told by a man that she cannot cope with the rigours of the world and to resist is to cruelly deprive him of looking after her properly.

Big Bio Brigade (BBB) is our way of describing the highly vocal, mainly male contingent of scientists who vigorously push the idea that men are *biologically* different from (and superior to) women. Most draw on evolutionary psychology for evidence of this.

Bro is a term used to indicate a certain kind of predominantly male arrogant and entitled behaviour. *Note*: This is a very White and privileged version of 'bro' – not the one adopted within Black male communities where it is an affectionate term, meaning 'my brother' in a broad sense.

Bropriation is the tendency for bros to appropriate resources from women, whether it be theories, good ideas, or simply control of a conversation.

Cisgenderism is where a person sees themselves as having the same gender identity that they were assigned at birth.

Decolonisation is an invective to act as well as a process of recognising the widespread impact of historical empire and imperialism, mostly by European countries, and of countering the continuing colonisation of the **minority world** by the **majority world**. A good resource in psychology is Glen Jankowski's BME Psychology project (https://bmepsychology.com/about/).

Default Man is a term invented by the artist Grayson Perry (2017) to describe what he calls 'a tribe' of men who are White, heterosexual, and, in particular, come from privileged backgrounds. He chose the word 'default' because it alludes to 'not having to pay their way' and 'being able to evade responsibility'. This tribe, he says, have a virtual monopoly on the high-status, high-earning jobs, and, more generally, 'set the rules' in ways that enable them to benefit from their privilege. They gain this power, he says, through the combination of an expensive education, good manners, charm, confidence, and sexual attractiveness. It is a particular version of **hegemonic masculinity**, but more concerned with entitlement than gender.

Discourse refers to the manner in which we speak and communicate about a certain topic. It can also refer to how social concepts are situated and constructed by such communication.

Empowerment in feminist terms is where women gain in confidence and self-worth, enabling them to bring changes in their circumstances. An excellent illustration is E.J. Renold's piece in Chapter 9, describing how schoolgirls had enormous fun with her making graffitied 'ruler skirts' as a way to stop boys at school 'upskirting' them.

Epistemology is essentially the 'theory of knowledge', the guiding philosophy underpinning what can be known, from a particular standpoint. The epistemology of experimental psychology tends to be positivist, whereas withthat of critical psychology it is social constructionist.

Fa'afāfine is a Samoan word used in Aotearoa/New Zealand which translates as 'in the manner of a woman'.

Fakaleiti is the Tongan term.

Female modesty effect is where women behave in a modest, unassuming way, in order not to be seen as 'uppity', 'too big for her boots', or just plain boastful. Women are constantly subjected to powerful social pressures not to come across as arrogant.

Feminist consciousness is a state of being in which you look at the social world around you from a feminist perspective – a cynical and suspicious viewpoint, always questioning whether power is being exercised. Its positive side is a consciousness where you revel in the warm support and encouragement of other women and your feminist allies and what you can achieve together.

Feminist killjoy – Sara Ahmed (2010, 2016) argues that we must have the courage to call out misbehaviour, even when this involves becoming a 'feminist killjoy'. You can learn a lot more on her website (which goes by the same name).

Gaslighting is a malicious strategy for exerting coercive control. It is often a long-term campaign by which mostly but not exclusively men gradually convince mostly but not exclusively women that they are 'going mad' and cannot trust their own thinking.

Governmentality describes the ways in which certain people are coerced by the powerful, and by the exercise of power, to comply with the rules being imposed at that time and in that place. Originally used by Michel Foucault, its most important proponent with regard to psychology is Nikolas Rose (1989), who identified psychology as *the* discipline in the social sciences that engages most in regulating and controlling people (see also ***psi complex***).

Global majority is a term adopted by Rosemary Campbell Stephens. She defines it thus: 'Global Majority is a collective term that first and foremost speaks to and encourages those so-called to think of themselves as belonging to the global majority. It refers to people who are and identify as, Black, African, Asian, Brown, Arab, dual-heritage, indigenous to the global south, and/or have been racialised as "ethnic minorities"'. It has recently been adopted in the UK as a better term than BAME, person of colour, or visible minorities. It links very well to our use of ***majority/minority worlds***. See more at: https://independent.academia.edu/RosemaryCampbellStephens.

Habitus is a term coined by Pierre Bourdieu, who defines it as 'a socially constituted system of cognitive and motivating structures' through which we present ourselves to the world. It is, he said, a 'durable manner of standing, speaking and thereby of feeling and thinking' that marks the person out as, say, working class, middle class, or an aristocrat (Bourdieu,

1990, p. 70). It is an ingrained aspect of our human embodiment – the bodily form of our being-in-the-world.

Hegemonic masculinity is the kind of masculinity that is promoted by **patriarchy** – the image of a 'real man' who is strong, masterful, all-capable, and brave. It is a hard act to follow, and causes considerable distress to men and boys generally. However, it needs to be noted that it is also the basis of much male power, with harmful impacts on both men and women and the way our society is run.

Her-story is a neat way of drawing attention to the fact that most history we know about and were taught at school was written by men and is a masculinist version of what happened and who matters. To explore *her*-stories is to look for and open up the stories that women have told, sometimes by pretending to be men.

Heteronormativity is about viewing heterosexuality as the only 'normal' way to be (and, by implication, assuming everything else is deviant in some way). It is a form of **Othering** and can harm anyone who cannot 'fit in'.

Hyper-feminine forms of consumption – Angela McRobbie (2009) adopted this term to describe the way all sorts of technologies, products, and services are offered to women to help them to 'improve' their looks – skin bleaching for being too coloured/tanning for being too pale; waxing and shaving to control body hair; manicures to make fingernails ornamental. Within a **neoliberal** system where the profit motive is all-important, women are persuaded that they are letting themselves go if they aren't constantly maintaining their bodies in a highly glamorised way.

Individualising is a term used in critical psychology to indicate that a particular concept, description, or theory is distorting, because it focuses solely on what goes on in individual minds, largely ignoring the way that so much of human life and experience so often is affected by the social and collective.

Infantilising is a particular form of **sexism** whereby women (usually) are regarded as if they were children who are incapable of adult maturity in order to control, denigrate, or exploit them.

Infrahumanisation is a form of dehumanisation – to be so hideously prejudiced against a group of people that they are (quite literally) denied their humanity and are instead viewed as 'less than' human. Regarding people as non-human acts as a justification for treating them without any empathy for their feelings or concerns about their welfare.

Institutional racism is a term adopted by Redi Eddo-Lodge, who defines it as 'dozens, or hundreds, or thousands of people with the same biases joining up together to make up one organisation, and acting accordingly'

(2017). It is a very useful term – as she herself says, '*Structural* is often the only way to capture what goes on unnoticed – the silently raised eyebrows, the implicit biases, snap judgements made on perceptions of competency' (2020, p. 64). This is very different from what is popularly understood as racism – overt hostility and antagonism to others, based on race. It is a much more subtle and insidious kind of racism. While it may not be intentional, it still has a very powerful effect, all the more problematic in that it can be invisible to everyone but its targets.

Intersectionality is a term which derives from Black feminist ideas and describes how our social identities exist within 'interlocking systems of oppression' and structures of (in)equalities (Crenshaw, 1991). It highlights how intersecting oppressed identities carry with them certain social expectations and norms. Importantly, intersectionality is rooted in a concern for social justice, stigma, and structural oppression, all of which are cornerstones of feminist social psychology.

Majority world is the term suggested by Shahidul Alam as a better alternative to terms like the 'Third World' or the 'developing world'. These are the people who have to cope with the economic and social impact of imperialism and colonialism, in contrast to the **minority world** where, as the colonisers, their exploitation has made them richer and better resourced. By using a different kind of binary, it shifts the moral emphasis in thought-provoking ways.

Manosphere is a world (mostly on the Internet) where men band together to troll and otherwise upset and undermine women.

Mansplaining is generally understood as the way in which some men automatically go into 'explain-mode' in conversation with a woman, ignoring the possibility that she does not need (or want) one, and, indeed, may well know a lot more about and understand the topic better! In our experience, it often happens without conscious thought or intention to belittle the woman concerned – but nonetheless it is a form of misogyny. However, for some men it can almost become a form of deliberate defiance, when, so determined is he to display his authority, it can come over as very confrontational – as many women, for example, experience when they gain high-end qualifications like a PhD.

Male gaze is a term used by Laura Mulvey (1975), a feminist film theorist, to describe the way in which films tend to be made from a highly masculinist perspective.

Malestream is a tongue-in-cheek version of 'mainstream', used by feminists to highlight just how male-dominated the mainstream is.

Manterrupting is used by feminists to draw attention to the propensity of men to constantly interrupt women in conversation and speak over them.

#MeToo movement is a social movement taking action against sexual abuse and sexual harassment. It started as an act of solidarity when women across the world declared that they too had been subjected to rape or sexual harassment. As the numbers of people signed up grew, it helped people to realise just how often women (and sometimes men) have been victims of sexual attacks. Tarana Burke began using the phrase "Me Too" in 2006 to raise awareness. Eleven years later, it found global recognition after a viral tweet by actress Alyssa Milano, accusing Hollywood producer Harvey Weinstein of sexual assault.

Minority world is a term we use to refer to what we often call the 'industrialised world', 'the West', or even the 'First World' – as opposed to the 'Developing World' and even the 'Third World'. The term 'minority world' was suggested by Shahidul Alam as a better and more respectful alternative. The term 'minority' highlights that it is not a matter of 'development' from a primitive to a civilised state, but more the economic and social impact of imperialism and colonialism (see **majority world**).

Missy is a recently constructed female identity in South Korea, where the identity of a modest, retiring wife and mother (in the past the only one available once a woman has married) is being resisted. A 'Missy' is a progressive, modern, and stylish woman free to follow fashion and to progress her own life opportunities. This identity was created initially through advertising but now is being promoted by women themselves as a form of resistance. We include it as an example of the way social change alters the kinds of identity that can be claimed.

Motherhood penalty is the cost that women pay for having children, mainly in terms of their career progression but also more generally in terms of engagement with the world beyond childcare. In countries that provide both men and women with childcare leave, the situation is much better.

'Mules and donkeys' is the term that Black women professors used to describe their career experiences in a study by Nicola Rollock (2019). It conveys very well the uphill battles they need to fight, and the sense they have of being doubly discriminated against, by being both women and Black.

Neoliberalism is a broad and complex **worldview**, although the term is somewhat obscure and very slippery. Unfortunately, many people rubbish it as pretentious and rather meaningless. It is the 'best of a bad job'; attempts to give us something better have floundered. Neoliberalism allows us to talk about a set of assumptions, ideas, and values that most certainly matter to our understanding of human life-worlds in the twenty-first century. It is predominantly based on the economic theory that competition is the key to human progress and prosperity, and hence that commerce is best practised through striving for the greatest level of profitability without having any conscience about its impact on the people it exploits. This philosophy soon expanded to include the public sector, viewing the provision of welfare services as also more functional when based upon competition. Its reach has been enormous, and, in our view, it poses a severe threat to the sustainability of humankind and our planet.

Neurofeminism is a feminist 'take' on the world of neuroscience. It challenges the ways in which neuroscience regards women's brains as biologically different from (and inferior to) men's brains (see Hoffman and Bluhm, 2016).

Neurosexism is the sexist way neuroscientists assume the above. The paper cited is also a useful resource here.

Objectification is where women get perceived as quite *literally* more object-like and less human than men (Heflick & Goldenberg, 2014). As Zaslow (2009) puts in, women are 'turned into an object to be consumed by men'.

Open Science Collaboration is a new paradigm in psychology's research providing innovative strategies to scrutinise the scientific quality of different research methodologies, designs, and the nature of the data obtained. The shift in values of the Open Science movement is particularly relevant for feminists, as it enables us to look closely at claims of innate sex differences.

Othering is when one group, 'us', constructs another group as 'not us'. It is not just about them being different, but 'less-than-us' or 'worse than' us in some way – less capable, not worth anything, not deserving of our kindness or concern. It is an antagonism that used to justify discrimination, disrespect, mistreatment, or undermining of the Other. It matters because it is a social process, in which people egg each other on, whipping up antagonism and vitriol.

Patriarchy is a **worldview** which sustains and maintains the historical power by which heterosexual men's interests dominate the way the social world works. This is *not* to claim that there is a deliberately devious and malignant male conspiracy going on. It is more complex than that, and more insidious. Patriarchy is a complicated system of interwoven ideas, assumptions, practices, and relationships, based on a particular understanding of the nature of human *being* – a patriarchal view of masculinity and femininity and the different functions and roles, expectations and entitlements, of men and women, girls and boys.

Perjurated means to strip a word of its value, and diminish its purpose. A good example is the way 'master' is a powerful and vigorous character; whereas 'mistress' is a more frivolous and inconsequential creature altogether.

Physics envy is a delicious way of being rude about those psychologists who desperately want to be 'hard' scientists, with all the bravura and credibility that offers. You can work out the connection to penis envy for yourself.

Post-feminism is, according to Ros Gill (2007), not so much a backlash against feminism or a later stage after it, but a phenomenon in itself – a consciousness of operating within different rules altogether. Under post-feminism, for example, the **male gaze** may be replaced by greater scrutiny coming from other women.

Protective paternalism is at the core of benevolent **sexism**. Offering help is at the heart of protective paternalism and, albeit maybe well-intentioned, undermines the autonomy of women (Nadler & Halabi, 2006).

Psy complex – Nikolas Rose (1989) adopted this terminology to categorise together psychologists, psychiatrists, and people in various counselling and other 'helping' roles (we think he would now include roles like life-coaching and motivational speakers). His concern is with the way this group of professionals have developed governmental systems – strategies, practices, and, more recently, technologies designed to resolve social problems (like criminality and mental distress), to manage performance (like staff recruitment and setting performance targets), and to enable people to live healthier and more productive lives. In so doing, he argues, this group acts as a powerful force for getting people to comply with regulatory regimes, many of which undermine human welfare.

Queer theory – Damien Riggs and Gareth Treharne (2017) define queer theory as a broad approach that contests the assumption that gender and sexuality are merely matters of individual identity or 'choice', and, instead, seeks to explore the multifaceted ways in which both are governed, constructed, managed, and performed. They draw extensively on the work of Judith Butler (1993).

Reflexivity is the process of deeply engaging in a form of self-reflection about who we are as researchers, how our biases guide and inform the research process, and how our **worldview** is shaped by the research we do (Wilkinson, 1988).

Sealioning is the act of intruding on and trying to derail a conversation with disingenuous questions (Kirkham, 2017).

Self-objectification is where a woman's consciousness is so distorted by patriarchal pressures that she perceives herself as an object of the **male gaze** and buys into its assumptions about her embodiment – that her brain is less capable than a man's and she is thus less intelligent.

Sexism is any statement or action hostile to women and girls, intended to denigrate, humiliate, belittle, and control them. It comes in many guises (see Chapter 5 for much more detail).

Slam poetry combines the elements of performance, writing, competition, and audience participation. The term 'slam' refers to its high-energy performance style. It's popular in the US and is slowly making its way over to the UK poetry scene too.

Social justice is based on the principle that everyone should be treated justly and equitably (but not necessarily the same). It is an approach that seeks to address issues like poverty, inequality, and injustice.

Systemic subordination – interpersonal theories of prejudice often position prejudice as something that occurs on a targeted, localised level, rather than being the product of something altogether larger and more systemic. This prejudice derives broadly from schemas – referred to by DiMaggio (1997) as a pattern of behaviour which acts as a framework and representation of our *worldview*.

TERFs or trans-exclusionary radical feminists – that is, feminists who are antagonistic towards trans women, seeing them as a threat to women's safety if they are allowed to penetrate into women-only spaces.

Testeria is a term adopted by feminists as counter to the use of 'hysteria' to define women's behaviour as melodramatically deranged. We find it a useful term to describe the frenzied attacks by INCELs and the like against any criticism of **hegemonic masculinity**.

Troubled identities are identities that are in some way problematised. Roper and Capdevila (2020) apply this term to stepmothers who, traditionally, are seen as wicked and dangerous. This situation requires the woman concerned to do 'identity work' to redeem herself.

Unconscious bias is biases, prejudices, or stereotypes that we hold about other groups that lies beneath our conscious awareness. This is sometimes referred to as 'implicit bias' and is thought to be measured through tasks such as implicit association tests.

Worldview is the term we generally use throughout this Companion to talk about the complex network of interconnected ideas, concepts, and beliefs that constitute common wisdom – what everybody knows – about a particular topic at a particular time and in a particular place. In many ways, though, terms like 'matrix of intelligibility' (taken from Judith Butler, 1993) is better at capturing the subtlety, complexity, and sheer scope of what is being talked about.

References

Aapola, S., Gonick, M., & Harris, A. (2005). *Young femininity: Girlhood, power, and social change*. London: Red Globe Press.

Abma, J. C., & Martinez, G. M. (2006). Childlessness among older women in the United States: Trends and profiles. *Journal of Marriage and Family, 68*(4), 1045–1056.

Ackerly, B., & True, J. (2008). Reflexivity in practice: Power and ethics in feminist research on international relations. *International Studies Review, 10*(4), 693–707.

Adams, V. H., III, Devos, T., Rivera, L. M., Smith, H., & Vega, L. A. (2014). Teaching about implicit prejudices and stereotypes: A pedagogical demonstration. *Teaching of Psychology, 41*(3), 204–212.

Advance Higher Education (2018). *Advance HE staff statistical report 2018: In brief*. Available at: https://blogs.ucl.ac.uk/astrea-blog/2018/11/30/advance_he_staff_stats_report_in_brief/.

Ahmed, S. (2010). Feminist killjoys. In *The promise of happiness* (pp. 50–87). Durham, NC: Duke University Press.

Ahmed, S. (2016). *Living a feminist life*. Durham, NC: Duke University Press.

Ahmed, S., & Bonis, O. (2012). Feminist killjoys (and other willful subjects). *Cahiers du Genre, 2*(53), 77–98.

Allen, K. R., & Jaramillo-Sierra, A. L. (2015). Feminist theory and research on family relationships: Pluralism and complexity. *Sex Roles, 73*(3), 93–99.

Ansara, Y. G., & Hegarty, P. (2013). Misgendering in English language contexts: Applying non-cisgenderist methods to feminist research. *International Journal of Multiple Research Approaches, 7*(2), 160–177.

Aronson, E., & Mills, J. (1959). The effect of severity of initiation on liking for a group. *Journal of Abnormal and Social Psychology, 59*(2), 177–181.

Atkinson, J.M., & Drew, P. (eds.) (1979). *Order in court: The organization of verbal interaction in judicial settings*. London: Social Sciences Research Council.

Badgett, M. V. L., & Folbre, N. (2003). Job gendering: Occupational choice and the marriage market. *Industrial Relations: A Journal of Economy and Society, 42*(2), 270–298.

Bagilhole, B., & Cross, S. (2006). 'It never struck me as female': Investigating men's entry into female-dominated occupations. *Journal of Gender Studies, 15*(1), 35–48.

Bailey, A. H., LaFrance, M., & Dovidio, J. F. (2020). Implicit androcentrism: Men are human, women are gendered. *Journal of Experimental Social Psychology, 89*, 103980. Available at: https://doi.org/10.1016/j.jesp.2020.103980.

Bailey, L. (1999). Refracted selves: A study of changes in self-identity in the transition to motherhood. *Sociology, 33*(2), 335–352.

Barclay, L., Everitt, L., Rogan, F., Schmied, V., & Wyllie, A. (1997). Becoming a mother – an analysis of women's experience of early motherhood. *Journal of Advanced Nursing, 25*(4), 719–728.

Barreto, M., & Ellemers, N. (2005). The burden of benevolent sexism: How it contributes to the maintenance of gender inequalities. *European Journal of Social Psychology, 35*(5), 633–642.

Bates, L. (2016). *Everyday sexism: The project that inspired a worldwide movement*. Basingstoke: Macmillan.

Becker, J. C., Zawadzki, M. J., & Shields, S. A. (2014). Confronting and reducing sexism: A call for research on intervention. *Journal of Social Issues, 70*(4), 603–614.

Bem, S. L. (1981). Gender schema theory: A cognitive account of sex typing. *Psychological Review, 88*(4), 354–364.

Benard, S., & Correll, S. J. (2010). Normative discrimination and the motherhood penalty. *Gender & Society, 24*(5), 616–646.

Bindman, J., & Doezema, J. (1997). *Redefining prostitution as sex work on the international agenda*. Available at: https://www.walnet.org/csis/papers/redefining.html.

Blackwell, A. L. B. (1875). *The sexes throughout nature*. New York: G.P. Putnam's.

Bleier, R. (1978). Bias in biological and human sciences: Some comments. *Signs: Journal of Women in Culture and Society, 4*(1), 159–162.

Blum, L. M., & Stracuzzi, N. F. (2004). Gender in the Prozac nation: Popular discourse and productive femininity. *Gender & Society, 18*(3), 269–286.

Bohan, J. S. (1993). Regarding gender: Essentialism, constructionism, and feminist psychology. *Psychology of Women Quarterly, 17*(1), 5–21.

Böhme, H. (2014). *Fetishism and culture: A different theory of modernity*. Berlin: Walter de Gruyter.

Bosson, J. K., & Vandello, J. A. (2011). Precarious manhood and its links to action and aggression. *Current Directions in Psychological Science, 20*(2), 82–86.

Bourdieu, P. (1990). *The logic of practice*. Cambridge: Polity Press.

Braun, V., & Clarke, V. (2019). Reflecting on reflexive thematic analysis. *Qualitative Research in Sport, Exercise and Health, 11*(4), 589–597.

Brizendine, L. (2007). *The female brain*. London: Bantam Books.

Burr, V. (2015). *Social constructivism* (3rd edition). London: Routledge.

Buss, D. M. (2016). *The evolution of desire: Strategies of human mating*. New York: Basic Books.

Butler, J. (1993). Critically queer. *GLQ: A Journal of Lesbian and Gay Studies, 1*(1), 17–32.

Cairns, K. (1993). Sexual entitlement and sexual accommodation: Male and female responses to sexual coercion. *Canadian Journal of Human Sexuality, 2*: 203–214.

Calogero, R. M. (2013). Objects don't object: Evidence that self-objectification disrupts women's social activism. *Psychological Science, 24*(3), 312–318.

Cameron, D. (1998). Performing gender identity: Young men's talk and the construction of heterosexual masculinity, in J. Coates (ed.) *Language and gender: A reader* (pp. 47–64). New York: Wiley.

Capdevila, R. and Frith, H. (forthcoming). *A feminist companion to research methods in psychology*. Feminist Companions to Psychology Series. London: Open University Press.

Carlson, E. R., & Carlson, R. (1960). Male and female subjects in personality research. *Journal of Abnormal and Social Psychology, 61*(3), 482–483.

Chafetz, J. S. (2004). Bridging feminist theory and research methodology. *Journal of Family Issues, 25*(7), 953–967.

Chambers, C. (2019). *The seven deadly sins of psychology: A manifesto for reforming the culture of scientific practice*. Princeton, NJ: Princeton University Press.

Chrisler, J. C. (2012). 'Why can't you control yourself?' Fat should be a feminist issue. *Sex Roles, 66*(9/10), 608–616.

Cialdini, R. B., & Trost, M. R. (1998). Social influence: Social norms, conformity and compliance, in D. T. Gilbert, S. T. Fiske, & G. Lindzey (eds.) *The handbook of social psychology* (Vol. 2, pp. 151–192). New York: McGraw-Hill.

Clarke, V., & Braun, V. (2019). Feminist qualitative methods and methodologies in psychology: A review and reflection. *Psychology of Women and Equalities Section Review, 2*(1), 13–28.

Coleman, R., Page, T., & Palmer, H. (2019). Introduction. Feminist new materialist practice: The mattering of methods. *MAI: Feminism & Visual Culture, 4*, 1–10.

Collins, P. H. (2000). *Black feminist thought: Knowledge, consciousness, and the politics of empowerment* (2nd edition). New York: Routledge.

Comas-Díaz, L. (1991). Feminism and diversity in psychology: The case of women of color. *Psychology of Women Quarterly, 15*(4), 597–609.

Condor, S. (1986). Sex role beliefs and "traditional" women: Feminist and intergroup perspectives, in S. Wilkinson (ed.) *Feminist social psychology: Developing theory and practice* (pp. 97–118). Milton Keynes: Open University Press.

Cranney, J., Morris, S., Martin, F. H., Provost, S., Zinkiewicz, L., Reece, J. et al. (2011). Psychological literacy and applied psychology in undergraduate education, in J. Cranney & D. S. Dunn (eds.) *The psychologically literate citizen: Foundations and global perspectives* (pp. 146–164). Oxford: Oxford University Press.

Crawford, M. (1995). *Talking difference: On gender and language.* London: Sage.

Crawford, M., & Marecek, J. (1989). Psychology reconstructs the female: 1968–1988. *Psychology of Women Quarterly, 13*(2), 147–165.

Crawford, M., & Unger, R.K. (eds.) (1997). *In our own words: Readings on the psychology of women and gender.* New York: McGraw-Hill.

Crawford, M., & Unger, R.K. (eds.) (2000). *In our own words: Writings from women's lives* (2nd edition). New York: McGraw-Hill.

Crenshaw, K. (1991). Mapping the margins: Identity politics, intersectionality, and violence against women. *Stanford Law Review, 43*(6), 1241–1299.

Criado-Perez. C. (2019). The deadly truth about a world built for men – from stab vests to car crashes. *Guardian,* 23 February.

Cross, C. P., Copping, L. T., & Campbell, A. (2011). Sex differences in impulsivity: A meta-analysis. *Psychological Bulletin, 137*(1), 97–130.

Cross, C. P., Cyrenne, D. L. M., & Brown, G. R. (2013). Sex differences in sensation-seeking: A meta-analysis. *Scientific Reports, 3*(1), 1–5.

Cross, S., & Bagilhole, B. (2002). Girls' jobs for the boys? Men, masculinity and non-traditional occupations. *Gender, Work & Organization, 9*(2), 204–226

Cuddy, A. J., Fiske, S. T., & Glick, P. (2007). The BIAS map: Behaviors from intergroup affect and stereotypes. *Journal of Personality and Social Psychology, 92*(4), 631–648.

Cuddy, A. J., Fiske, S. T., Kwan, V. S., Glick, P., Demoulin, S., Leyens, J. P. et al. (2009). Stereotype content model across cultures: Towards universal similarities and some differences. *British Journal of Social Psychology, 48*(1), 1–33.

Daly, M. (1978). The cost of mating. *American Naturalist, 112*(986), 771–774.

Davey, M. (2019). One in seven young Australians say rape is justified if women change their mind, study finds. *Guardian,* 21 June.

Davidson, J. (1984). Subsequent versions of invitations, offers, requests, and proposals: Dealing with potential or actual rejection, in J.M. Atkinson & J. Heritage (eds.) *Structures of social action: Studies in conversation analysis* (pp. 102–128). Cambridge: Cambridge University Press.

Day, K., Gough, B., & McFadden, M. (2004). 'Warning! Alcohol can seriously damage your feminine health': A discourse analysis of recent British newspaper coverage of women and drinking. *Feminist Media Studies, 4*(2), 165–183.

de Beauvoir, S. (1949/1997). *The second sex.* London: Vintage.

D'Ignazio, C., & Klein, L. F. (2020). *Data feminism.* Boston, MA: MIT Press.

DiMaggio, P. (1997). Culture and cognition. *Annual Review of Sociology, 23*(1), 263–287.

Douglas, S., & Michaels, M. (2005). *The mommy myth: The idealization of motherhood and how it has undermined all women.* New York: Simon & Schuster.

Driscoll, C. (1999). Girl culture, revenge and global capitalism: Cybergirls, riot grrls, spice girls. *Australian Feminist Studies, 14*(29), 173–193.

Dutt, A., & Grabe, S. (2014). Lifetime activism, marginality, and psychology: Narratives of lifelong feminist activists committed to social change. *Qualitative Psychology, 1*(2), 107–122.

Eagly, A. H. (2012). Bias, feminism, and the psychology of investigating gender, in R. W. Proctor & E. J. Capaldi (eds.) *Psychology of science: Implicit and explicit processes* (pp. 267–288). Oxford: Oxford University Press.

Eagly, A. H., & Diekman, A. B. (2005). What is the problem? Prejudice as an attitude-in-context, in J.F. Dovidio, P. Glick, & L. A. Rudman (eds.) *On the nature of prejudice: Fifty years after Allport* (pp. 19–35). Oxford: Blackwell.

Eagly, A. H., & Mladinic, A. (1994). Are people prejudiced against women? Some answers from research on attitudes, gender stereotypes, and judgments of competence. *European Review of Social Psychology, 5*(1), 1–35.

Eagly, A. H., & Riger, S. (2014). Feminism and psychology: Critiques of methods and epistemology. *American Psychologist, 69*(7), 685–702.

Eagly, A. H., & Wood, W. (2011). Feminism and the evolution of sex differences and similarities. *Sex Roles, 64*(9/10), 758–767.

Eagly, A. H., Eaton, A., Rose, S. M., Riger, S., & McHugh, M. C. (2012). Feminism and psychology: Analysis of a half-century of research on women and gender. *American Psychologist, 67*(3), 211–230.

Ebert, I. D., Steffens, M. C., & Kroth, A. (2014). Warm, but maybe not so competent? Contemporary implicit stereotypes of women and men in Germany. *Sex Roles, 70*(9/10), 359–375.

Eddo-Lodge, R. (2017). Why I'm no longer talking to white people about race. *Guardian,* 30 May.

Eddo-Lodge, R. (2020). *Why I'm no longer talking to white people about race.* London: Bloomsbury.

Elliot, A. J., & Pazda, A. D. (2012). Dressed for sex: Red as a female sexual signal in humans, *PLoS One, 7*(4), e34607. Available at: https://doi.org/10.1371/journal.pone.0034607.

Enloe, C. (2017). *The big push: Exposing and challenging the persistence of patriarchy.* Stanford, CA: University of California Press.

Fausto-Sterling, A. (2000). Beyond difference: Feminism and evolutionary psychology, in H. Rose & S. Rose (eds.) *Alas, poor Darwin: Arguments against evolutionary psychology* (pp. 209–227). London: Jonathan Cape.

Fausto-Sterling, A. (2008). *Myths of gender: Biological theories about women and men.* New York: Basic Books.

Feingold, A. (1994). Gender differences in personality: A meta-analysis. *Psychological Bulletin, 116*(3), 429–456.

Ferguson, M. A., Branscombe, N. R., & Reynolds, K. J. (2019). Social psychological research on prejudice as collective action supporting emergent ingroup members. *British Journal of Social Psychology, 58*(1), 1–32.

Fine, C. (2008). Will working mothers' brains explode? The popular new genre of neurosexism. *Neuroethics, 1*(1), 69–72.

Fine, C. (2010). *Delusions of gender: How our minds, society, and neurosexism create difference.* New York: W. W. Norton.

Fine, C. (2012). Explaining, or sustaining, the status quo? The potentially self-fulfilling effects of 'hardwired' accounts of sex differences. *Neuroethics, 5*(3), 285–294.

Fine, M., & Gordon, S. M. (1991). Effacing the center and the margins: Life at the intersection of psychology and feminism. *Feminism & Psychology, 1*(1), 19–27.

Fiske, S. T., Cuddy, A. J., & Glick, P. (2007). Universal dimensions of social cognition: Warmth and competence. *Trends in Cognitive Sciences, 11*(2), 77–83.

Fiske, S. T., Cuddy, A. J., Glick, P., & Xu, J. (2002). A model of (often mixed) stereotype content: Competence and warmth respectively follow from perceived status and competition. *Journal of Personality and Social Psychology, 82*(6), 878–902.

Flew, F., Bagilhole, B., Carabine, J., Fenton, N., Kitzinger, C., Lister, R. et al. (1999). Introduction: Local feminisms, global futures. *Women's Studies International Forum, 22*(4), 393–403.

Foucault, M. (1977). *Discipline and punish: The birth of the prison*, trans. A. Sheridan. London: Allen Lane.

Fredrickson, B. L., & Roberts, T. A. (1997). Objectification theory: Toward understanding women's lived experiences and mental health risks. *Psychology of Women Quarterly, 21*(2), 173–206.

Fredrickson, B. L., Roberts, T. A., Noll, S. M., Quinn, D. M., & Twenge, J. M. (1998). That swimsuit becomes you: Sex differences in self-objectification, restrained eating, and math performance. *Journal of Personality and Social Psychology, 75*(1), 269–284.

Friedan, B. (1963). *The feminine mystique.* New York: W. W. Norton.

Frith, H. (ed.) (2004). The best of friends: The politics of girls' friendships. Special issue of *Feminism & Psychology, 14*(3).

Gabb, J., Klett-Davies, M., Fink, J., & Thomae, M. (2013). *Enduring love? Couple relationships in the 21st century.* Survey Findings Report. Milton Keynes: The Open University.

Gangestad, S. W., & Buss, D. M. (1993). Pathogen prevalence and human mate preferences. *Ethology and Sociobiology, 14*(2), 89–96.

Gangestad, S. W., & Simpson, J. A. (2000). The evolution of human mating: Trade-offs and strategic pluralism. *Behavioral and Brain Sciences, 23*(4), 573–587.

Gavey, N. (1989). Feminist poststructuralism and discourse analysis: Contributions to feminist psychology. *Psychology of Women Quarterly, 13*(4), 459–475.

Gentles-Peart, K. (2020). 'Fearfully and wonderfully made': Black Caribbean women and the decolonization of thick Black female bodies. *Feminism & Psychology, 30*(3), 306–323.

Gergen, M. (2008). Qualitative methods in feminist psychology, in C. Willig & W. Stainton Rogers (eds.) *The Sage handbook of qualitative research in psychology* (pp. 280–295). London: Sage.

Gill, R. (2007). Postfeminist media culture: Elements of a sensibility. *European Journal of Cultural Studies, 10*(2), 147–166.

Gill, R., & Orgad, S. (2018). The amazing bounce-backable woman: Resilience and the psychological turn in neoliberalism. *Sociological Research Online, 23*(2), 477–495.

Gilligan, C. (1993). *In a different voice: Psychological theory and women's development.* Cambridge, MA: Harvard University Press.

Ging, D. (2019). Alphas, betas, and incels: Theorizing the masculinities of the manosphere. *Men and Masculinities, 22*(4), 638–657.

Glick, P., & Fiske, S. T. (2001). An ambivalent alliance: Hostile and benevolent sexism as complementary justifications for gender inequality. *American Psychologist, 56*(2), 109–118.

Glick, P. & Fiske, S. T. (2011). Ambivalent sexism revisited. *Psychology of Women Quarterly, 35*(3), 530–535.

Gluck, S., & Patai, D. (1991). Introduction, in S. Gluck & D. Patai (eds.) *Women's words: The feminist practice of oral history* (pp. 1–5). New York: Routledge.

Goins, M. N. (2011). Playing with dialectics: Black female friendship groups as a homeplace. *Communication Studies, 62*(5), 531–546.

Good, C., Rattan, A., & Dweck, C. S. (2012). Why do women opt out? Sense of belonging and women's representation in mathematics. *Journal of Personality and Social Psychology, 102*(4), 700–717.

Goodwin, C. J. (2010). *Research in psychology: Methods and design* (6th edition). New York: Wiley.

Gray, J. (1992). *Men are from Mars, women are from Venus.* London: Harper Thorsons.

Griffin, R. A. (2012). I AM an angry Black woman: Black feminist autoethnography, voice, and resistance. *Women's Studies in Communication, 35*(2), 138–157.

Grogan, S. (2016). *Body image: Understanding body dissatisfaction in men, women and children.* Abingdon: Routledge.

Hamaguchi, E. (1985). A contextual model of the Japanese: Toward a methodological innovation in Japan studies. *Journal of Japanese Studies, 11*(1), 289–321.

Haraway, D. (1986). Situated knowledges: The science question in feminism and the privilege of partial perspectives. *Feminist Studies, 14*(3), 575–599.

Hays, S. (1996). *The cultural contradictions of motherhood.* New Haven, CT: Yale University Press.

Heatherington, L., Daubman, K. A., Bates, C., Ahn, A., Brown, H., & Preston, C. (1993). Two investigations of 'female modesty' in achievement situations. *Sex Roles, 29*(11), 739–754.

Heflick, N. A., & Goldenberg, J. L. (2014). Seeing eye to body: The literal objectification of women. *Current Directions in Psychological Science, 23*(3), 225–229.

Heflick, N. A., Goldenberg, J. L., Cooper, D. P., & Puvia, E. (2011). From women to objects: Appearance focus, target gender, and perceptions of warmth, morality and competence. *Journal of Experimental Social Psychology, 47*(3), 572–581.

Heilman, M. E., & Wallen, A. S. (2010). Wimpy and undeserving of respect: Penalties for men's gender-inconsistent success. *Journal of Experimental Social Psychology, 46*(4), 664–667.

Henderson, A., Harmon, S., & Newman, H. (2016). The price mothers pay, even when they are not buying it: Mental health consequences of idealized motherhood. *Sex Roles, 74*(11/12), 512–526.

Henley, N., & Freeman, J. (1989). The sexual politics of interpersonal behavior, in J. Freeman (ed.) *Women: A feminist perspective* (4th edition, pp. 457–469). Mountain View, CA: Mayfield.

Henriques, J., Hollway, W., Urwin, C., Venn, C., & Walkerdine, V. (eds.) (1984). *Changing the subject: Psychology, social regulation, and subjectivity.* London: Methuen.

Herek, G. M. (2007). Confronting sexual stigma and prejudice: Theory and practice. *Journal of Social Issues, 63*(4), 905–925.

Herek, G. M., Kimmel, D. C., Amaro, H., & Melton, G. B. (1991). Avoiding heterosexist bias in psychological research. *American Psychologist, 44*(9), 957–963.

Hettinger, V. E., Hutchinson, D. M., & Bosson, J. K. (2014). Influence of professional status on perceptions of romantic relationship dynamics. *Psychology of Men & Masculinity, 15*(4), 470–480.

Hoffman, G. A., & Bluhm, R. (2016). Neurosexism and neurofeminism. *Philosophy Compass, 11*(11), 716–729.

Hogg, M. A., & Vaughan, G. M (2018). *Social Psychology* (8th edition). London: Pearson.

Holland, E., Koval, P., Stratemeyer, M., Thomson, F., & Haslam, N. (2017). Sexual objectification in women's daily lives: A smartphone ecological momentary assessment study. *British Journal of Social Psychology, 56*(2), 314–333.

Howell, T., & Allen, L. (2020). 'Good morning boys': Fa'afāfine and Fakaleiti experiences of cisgenderism at an all-boys secondary school. *Sex Education.* Available at: https://doi.org/10.1080/14681811.2020.1813701.

Hyers, L. L. (2007). Resisting prejudice every day: Exploring women's assertive responses to anti-Black racism, anti-Semitism, heterosexism, and sexism. *Sex Roles, 56*(1), 1–12.

James, W. (1907). Pragmatism's conception of truth. *Journal of Philosophy, Psychology and Scientific Methods, 4*(6), 141–155.

Jankowski, G. (2020). BME Psychology. Available at: www.bmepsychology.com.

Jankowski, G., Braun, V., & Clarke, V. (2017). Reflecting on qualitative research, feminist methodologies and feminist psychology: In conversation with Virginia Braun and Victoria Clarke. *Psychology of Women Section Review, 19*(1), 43–55.

Johnston, D. D., & Swanson, D. H. (2007). Cognitive acrobatics in the construction of worker–mother identity. *Sex Roles, 57*(5/6), 447–459.

Joyce, J. B., Humă, B., Ristimäki, H. L., Almeida, F. F. D., & Doehring, A. (2021). Speaking out against everyday sexism: Gender and epistemics in accusations of "mansplaining". *Feminism & Psychology*. Available at: https://doi.org/10.1177/0959353520979499.

Kahneman, D. (2011). *Thinking, fast and slow*. Basingstoke: Palgrave Macmillan.

Kasardo, A. E., & McHugh, M. C. (2015). From fat shaming to size acceptance: Challenging the medical management of fat women, in M. C. McHugh & J. C. Chrisler (eds.) *The wrong prescription for women: How medicine and media create a "need" for treatments, drugs, and surgery* (pp. 179–201). Santa Barbara, CA: Praeger.

Kemmis, S. (2006). Participatory action research and the public sphere. *Educational Action Research, 14*(4), 459–476.

Kim, J. M. (2011). Is 'the Missy' a new femininity?, in R. Gill & C. Scharff (eds.) *New femininities: Postfeminism, neoliberalism and subjectivity* (pp. 147–158). London: Palgrave Macmillan.

Kimmel, E. B. (1989). The experience of feminism. *Psychology of Women Quarterly, 13*(2), 133–146.

Kirkham, A. (2017). *Sealioning: How to deal with the time-wasting troll tactic we're all tired of*. Available at: https://everydayfeminism.com/2017/01/sealioning/.

Kitzinger, C. (ed.) (1994). Should psychologists study sex differences? Special issue of *Feminism & Psychology, 4*(4).

Kitzinger, C., & Frith, H. (1999). Just say no? The use of conversation analysis in developing a feminist perspective on sexual refusal. *Discourse & Society, 10*(3), 293–316.

Kitzinger, C., & Wilkinson, S. (1996). Theorizing representing the other, in S. Wilkinson & C. Kitzinger (eds.) *Representing the other: A feminism and psychology reader* (pp. 1–32). London: Sage.

Koudenburg, N., Kannegieter, A., Postmes, T., & Kashima, Y. (2020). The subtle spreading of sexist norms. *Group Processes & Intergroup Relations*. Available at: https://doi.org/10.1177/1368430220961838.

Kurtiş, T., & Adams, G. (2015). Decolonizing liberation: Toward a transnational feminist psychology. *Journal of Social and Political Psychology, 3*(1), 388–413.

Lakoff, R. T. (2004). *Language and woman's place: Text and commentaries* (revised and expanded edition). New York: Oxford University Press.

Lal, J., McGuire, K., Stewart, A. J., Zaborowska, M., & Pas, J. M. (2010). Recasting global feminisms: Toward a comparative historical approach to women's activism and feminist scholarship. *Feminist Studies, 36*(1), 13–39.

Langhorne, M. C., & Secord, P. F. (1955). Variations in marital needs with age, sex, marital status, and regional location. *Journal of Social Psychology, 41*(1), 19–37.

Langsted, O. (1994). Looking at quality from the child's perspective, in P. Moss & A. Pence (eds.) *Valuing quality in early childhood services: New approaches to defining quality* (pp. 28–42). London: Sage.

Lazard, L. (2020). *Sexual harassment, psychology and feminism: # MeToo, victim politics and predators in neoliberal times*. Basingstoke: Palgrave Macmillan.

Lazard, L., & McAvoy, J. (2020). Doing reflexivity in psychological research: What's the point? What's the practice? *Qualitative Research in Psychology, 17*(2), 159–177.

Lemish, D. (2003). Spice world: Constructing femininity the popular way. *Popular Music & Society, 26*(1), 17–29.

Lepore, J. (2011). Growing old and even older. *The New Yorker*, 6 March. Available at: https://www.newyorker.com/magazine/2011/03/14/twilight-jill-lepore.

Lewis, M. (1990). Interrupting patriarchy: Politics, resistance, and transformation in the feminist classroom. *Harvard Educational Review, 60*(4), 467–489.

Lewis, N. A., Jr ., & Wai, J. (2020). Communicating what we know, and what isn't so: Science communication in psychology. *Perspectives on Psychological Science*. Available at: https://doi.org/10.1177/1745691620964062.

Libby, Georgia, Chloe, Courtney, Olivia, & Rhiannon, with Renold, E. (2018). Making our feelings matters: Using creative methods to re-assemble the rules on healthy relationships education in Wales, in N. Lombard (ed.) *The Routledge handbook of gender and violence* (pp. 303–319). London: Taylor & Francis, pp. 303–319.

Lorber, J. (2000). Using gender to undo gender: A feminist degendering movement. *Feminist Theory, 1*(1), 79–95.

Lorde, A. (1984). The master's tools will never dismantle the master's house, in *Sister outsider: Essays and speeches* (pp. 110–114). Berkeley, CA: Crossing Press. Available at: https://collectiveliberation.org/wp-content/uploads/2013/01/Lorde_The_Masters_Tools.pdf.

Lott, B. (1991). Social psychology: Humanist roots and feminist future. *Psychology of Women Quarterly, 15*(4), 505–519.

Lubek, I., & Stam, H. J. (1995). Ludicro-experimentation in social psychology: Sober scientific versus playful prescriptions, in I. Lubek, R. van Hezewijk, G. Pheterson, & C. W. Tolman (eds.) *Trends and issues in theoretical psychology* (pp. 171–180). Berlin: Springer.

Lucas, S., & Beetham, T. (2019). *Peri-natal evaluation: Maternal mental wellbeing, Quarriers, Ruchazie*. Stirling: University of Stirling, Centre for Child Wellbeing and Protection.

MacArthur, H. J., & Shields, S. A. (2014). Psychology's feminist voices: A critical pedagogical tool. *Sex Roles, 70*(9/10), 431–433.

Maccoby, E. E., & Jacklin, C. N. (1974). Myth, reality and shades of gray: What we know and don't know about sex differences. *Psychology Today, 8*(7), 109–112.

Mackay, F. (2015). Introduction: Why march through this book?, in *Radical Feminism* (pp. 1–32). Basingstoke: Palgrave Macmillan.

Magnusson, E., & Marecek, J. (2012). *Gender and culture in psychology: Theories and practices*. Cambridge: Cambridge University Press.

Mahood, L., & Littlewood, B. (1997). Daughters in danger: The case of 'campus sex crimes', in A. M. Thomas & C. Kitzinger (eds.) *Sexual harassment: Contemporary feminist perspectives* (pp. 157–171). Milton Keynes: Open University Press.

Majors, R., & Billston, J. (1992). *Cool pose: The dilemmas of Black manhood in America*. New York: Lexington Books.

Mallet, R. K., & Wagner, D. E. (2011). The unexpectedly positive consequences of confronting sexism. *Journal of Experimental Social Psychology, 47*, 215–220.

Mann, S. A. (2012). *Doing feminist theory: From modernity to postmodernity*. Oxford: Oxford University Press.

Marecek, J. (2019). A history of the future: Carolyn Wood Sherif, equitable knowledge, and feminist psychology. *Psychology of Women Quarterly, 43*(4), 422–432.

Martin, C. L., & Ruble, D. (2004). Children's search for gender cues: Cognitive perspectives on gender development. *Current Directions in Psychological Science, 13*(2), 67–70.

Martin, J. L., & Smith, J. (2020, July/August). Why we march! Feminist activism in critical times: Lessons from the women's march on Washington, *Women's Studies International Forum*, 81, 102375. Available at: https://doi.org/10.1016/j.wsif.2020.102375.

Martin, K. A. (2005). William wants a doll: Can he have one? Feminists, child care advisors, and gender-neutral child rearing. *Gender & Society, 19*(4), 456–479.

Martinussen, M., Wetherell, M., & Braun, V. (2020). Just being and being bad: Female friendship as a refuge in neoliberal times. *Feminism & Psychology, 30*(1), 3–21.

Massumi, B. (2015) *Politics of affect*. New York: Wiley.

McDonald, J. (2013). Conforming to and resisting dominant gender norms: How male and female nursing students do and undo gender. *Gender, Work & Organization, 20*(5), 561–579.

McRobbie, A. (2009). *The aftermath of feminism: Gender, culture and social change*. London: Sage.

Mead, G. H. (1934). *Mind, self and society*. Chicago, IL: University of Chicago Press.

Miller, C., & Swift, K. (1976). *Words and women*. New York: Anchor Press.

Miller, K. (2020, August). Why I no longer wish to be associated with the BPS (Letter). *The Psychologist*.

Miller, T. (2007). 'Is this what motherhood is all about?' Weaving experiences and discourse through transition to first-time motherhood. *Gender & Society, 21*(3), 337–358.

Mohanty, C. (1988). Under Western eyes: Feminist scholarship and colonial discourses. *Feminist Review, 30*(1), 61–88.

Mol, A. (2008). *The logic of care: Health and the problem of patient choice*. London: Routledge.

Moss-Racusin, C. A., Dovidio, J. F., Brescoll, V. L., Graham, M. J., & Handelsman, J. (2012). Science faculty's subtle gender biases favor male students. *Proceedings of the National Academy of Sciences, 109*(41), 16474–16479.

Mott, C., & Cockayne, D. (2017). Citation matters: Mobilizing the politics of citation toward a practice of 'conscientious engagement'. *Gender, Place & Culture, 24*(7), 954–973.

Mulvey, L. (1975). Visual pleasure and narrative cinema. *Screen, 16*(3), 6–18.

Nadler, A., & Halabi, S. (2006). Intergroup helping as status relations: Effects of status stability, identification, and type of help on receptivity to high-status group's help. *Journal of Personality and Social Psychology, 91*(1), 97–110.

Nash, M. (2012). 'In-between' pregnant bodies, in *Making 'Postmodern' Mothers* (pp. 41–61). London: Palgrave Macmillan

Nickerson, R. S. (1998). Confirmation bias: A ubiquitous phenomenon in many guises. *Review of General Psychology, 2*(2), 175–220. https://doi.org/10.1037/1089-2680.2.2.175

Nier, J. A., & Campbell, S. D. (2013). Two outsiders' view on feminism and evolutionary psychology: An opportune time for adversarial collaboration. *Sex Roles, 69*(9/10), 503–506.

Ogle, J., Tyner, K. E., & Schofield-Tomschin, S. (2011). Jointly navigating the reclamation of the 'Woman I used to be': Negotiating concerns about the postpartum body within the marital dyad. *Clothing and Textiles Research Journal, 29*(1), 35–51.

Olson, C.B. (1988). The influence of context on gender differences in performance attributions: Further evidence of a 'feminine modesty' effect. Paper presented at the Meeting of the Western Psychological Association, San Francisco, CA.

Open Science Collaboration. (2015). Estimating the reproducibility of psychological science. *Science, 349*(6251): aac4716. Available at: https://doi.org/10.1126/science.aac4716.

Oswell, D. (2013). *The agency of children: From family to global human rights*. Cambridge: Cambridge University Press.

Perez, C. C. (2019). *Invisible women: Exposing data bias in a world designed for men*. New York: Random House.

Perry, G. (2017). *The descent of man*. London: Penguin.

Perry, G. (2019). *The lost boys: Inside Muzafer Sherif's Robbers Cave experiment*. London: Scribe.

Persson, S., & Pownall, M. (2021). Can Open Science be a tool to dismantle claims of hardwired brain sex differences? Opportunities and challenges for feminist researchers. *Psychology of Women Quarterly*.

Phelan, J. E., Moss-Racusin, C. A., & Rudman, L. A. (2008). Competent yet out in the cold: Shifting criteria for hiring reflect backlash toward agentic women. *Psychology of Women Quarterly, 32*(4), 406–413.

Phoenix, A., Frosh, S., & Pattman, R. (2003). Producing contradictory masculine subject positions: Narratives of threat, homophobia and bullying in 11–14 year old boys. *Journal of Social Issues, 59*(1), 179–195.

Pope, K. S., Levenson, H., & Schover, L. R. (1979). Sexual intimacy in psychology training: Results and implications of a national survey. *American Psychologist, 34*(8), 682–689.

Popp, D., Donovan, R., Crawford, M., Marsh, K., & Peele, M. (2003). Gender, race, and speech style stereotypes. *Sex Roles, 48*(7/8): 317–325.

Potter, J., & Wetherell, M. (1987). *Discourse and social psychology: Beyond attitudes and behaviour*. London: Sage.

Pullen, A., & Simpson, R. (2009). Managing difference in feminized work: Men, otherness and social practice. *Human Relations, 62*(4), 561–587.

Radtke, H.L. (2017). Feminist theory in *Feminism & Psychology* [Part I]: dealing with differences and negotiating the biological. *Feminism & Psychology, 27*(3), 357–377.

Raymond, J. G. (2001). *A passion for friends: Toward a philosophy of female affection*. North Melbourne: Spinifex Press.

Renold, E. (2005). *Girls, boys, and junior sexualities: Exploring children's gender and sexual relations in the primary school*. London: RoutledgeFalmer.

Renold, E. (2019). Ruler-skirt risings: Being crafty with how gender and sexuality education research-activisms can come to matter, in T. Jones, L. Coll, L. van Leent, & Y. Taylor (eds.) *Uplifting gender and sexuality education research* (pp. 115–140). Basingstoke: Palgrave Macmillan.

Renold, E.J., Ashton, M.R., & McGeeney, E. (2021). What if?: Becoming response-able with the making and mattering of a new relationships and sexuality education curriculum. *Professional Development in Education, 47*(2/3), 538–555.

Renold, E.J., & Timperley, V. (2021). Re-assembling the rules: Becoming creative with making 'youth voice' matter in the field of relationships and sexuality education, in D. Lupton and D. Leahy (eds.) *Creative approaches to health education*, London: Routledge.

Rich, A. (1980). Compulsory heterosexuality and lesbian existence. *Signs: Journal of Women in Culture and Society, 5*(4): 631–660.

Riggs, D. W., & Bartholomaeus, C. (2020). Toward trans reproductive justice: A qualitative analysis of views on fertility preservation for Australian transgender and non-binary people. *Journal of Social Issues, 76*(2), 314–337.

Riggs, D. W., & Treharne, G. J. (2017). Queer theory, in B. Gough (ed.) *The Palgrave handbook of critical social psychology* (pp. 101–121). London: Palgrave Macmillan.

Riley, S., Evans, A., & Mackiewicz, A. (2016). It's just between girls: Negotiating the postfeminist gaze in women's 'looking talk'. *Feminism & Psychology, 26*(1), 94–113.

Ringrose, J., & Walkerdine, V. (2008). Regulating the abject: The TV make-over as a site of neo-liberal reinvention toward bourgeois femininity. *Feminist Media Studies*, *8*(3), 227–246.

Rippon, G. (2019). *The gendered brain: The new neuroscience that shatters the myth of the female brain*. New York: Random House.

Rollock, N. (2019). *Staying power: The career experiences and strategies of UK Black female professors*. London: UCU. Available at: https://www.ucu.org.uk/media/10075/Staying-Power/pdf/UCU_Rollock_February_2019.pdf.

Roper, S., & Capdevila, R. (2020). Hapless, helpless, hopeless: An analysis of stepmothers' talk about their (male) partners. *Feminism & Psychology*, *30*(2), 248–266.

Rose, N. (1989). *Governing the soul: Shaping of the private self*. London: Free Association Books.

Rose, N., O'Malley, P., & Valverde, M. (2006). Governmentality. *Annual Review of Law and Social Science*, *2*, 83–104.

Rose, S., & Roades, L. (1987). Feminism and women's friendships. *Psychology of Women Quarterly*, *11*(2), 243–254.

Rosenthal, L. (2016). Incorporating intersectionality into psychology: An opportunity to promote social justice and equity. *American Psychologist*, *71*(6), 474–485.

Rudman, L. A., & Phelan, J. E. (2008). Backlash effects for disconfirming gender stereotypes in organizations. *Research in Organizational Behavior*, *28*, 61–79.

Russo, N. F. (1976). The motherhood mandate. *Journal of Social Issues*, *32*(3), 143–153.

Rutherford, A. (2007). V. Feminist questions, feminist answers: Towards a redefinition. *Feminism & Psychology*, *17*(4), 459–464.

Rutherford, A. (2021). *Psychology at the intersections of gender, feminism, history, and culture*. Cambridge: Cambridge University Press.

Rutherford, A., Vaughn-Blount, K., & Ball, L. C. (2010). Responsible opposition, disruptive voices: Science, social change, and the history of feminist psychology. *Psychology of Women Quarterly*, *34*(4), 460–473.

Ruti, M. (2015). *The age of scientific sexism: How evolutionary psychology promotes gender profiling and fans the battle of the sexes*. London: Bloomsbury.

Sabat, I. E., Lindsey, A. P., King, E. B., & Jones, K. P. (2016). Understanding and overcoming challenges faced by working mothers: A theoretical and empirical review, in C. Spitzmueller & R. A. Matthews (eds.) *Research perspectives on work and the transition to motherhood* (pp. 9–31). Dordrecht: Springer.

Saini, A. (2017). *Inferior: How science got women wrong and the new research that's rewriting the story*. Boston, MA: Beacon Press.

Saini, A. (2019). *Superior: The return of race science*. Boston, MA: Beacon Press.

Schmidt, J. (2016). Being 'like a woman': Fa'afāfine and Samoan masculinity. *Asia Pacific Journal of Anthropology*, *17*(3/4): 287–304.

Schmitz, S. (2010). Sex, gender, and the brain – biological determinism versus sociocultural constructivism, in I. Klinge & C. Wiesemann (eds.) *Sex and gender in biomedicine: Theories, methodologies, results* (pp. 57–76). Göttingen: Universitätsverlag Göttingen.

Shahvisi, A. (2020). Nesting behaviours during pregnancy: Biological instinct, or another way of gendering housework? *Women's Studies International Forum*, 78, 102329. Available at: https://doi.org/10.1016/j.wsif.2019.102329.

Sharma, S. (2018). I don't feel like a woman, in S. Curtis (curator), *Feminists don't wear pink and other lies*. London: Penguin Books.

Sherif, C. W. (1998). Bias in psychology. *Feminism & Psychology*, *8*(1), 58–75.

Sherif, M. (1954). *Experimental study of positive and negative intergroup attitudes between experimentally produced groups: Robbers Cave study*. Norman, OK: University of Oklahoma.

Shiebinger, L. (1991). *The mind has no sex? Women in the origins of modern science.* Cambridge, MA: Harvard University Press.

Singh, D. (2006). Universal allure of the hourglass figure: An evolutionary theory of female physical attractiveness. *Clinics in Plastic Surgery, 33*(3), 359–370.

Singleton, P. (2020). Remodelling Barbie, making justice: An autoethnography of craftivist encounters. *Feminism & Psychology.* Available at: https://doi.org/10.1177/0959353520941355.

Skeggs, B. (2005). The making of class and gender through visualizing moral subject formation. *Sociology, 39*(5), 965–982.

Smith, C. A., & Konik, J. A. (eds.) (2011). Feminism and evolutionary psychology. Special issue of *Sex Roles, 64*(9/10).

Solnit, R. (2014). *Men explain things to me.* London: Haymarket Books.

Spender, D. (1985). *Man made language* (2nd edition). London: Pandora.

Sprott, W. J. H. (1952). *Social psychology.* London: Methuen.

Stake, J. E. (2007). Predictors of change in feminist activism through women's and gender studies. *Sex Roles, 57*(1/2), 43–54.

Stanley, J. (1973). Paradigmatic woman: The prostitute. Paper presented to the Linguistic Society of America.

Stokoe, E. H. (2000). IV. Toward a conversation analytic approach to gender and discourse. *Feminism & Psychology, 10*(4), 552–563.

Stoudt, B. G., Fox, M., & Fine, M. (2012). Contesting privilege with critical participatory action research. *Journal of Social Issues, 68*(1), 178–193.

Sutton, R. M., Douglas, K. M., & McClellan, L. M. (2011). Benevolent sexism, perceived health risks, and the inclination to restrict pregnant women's freedoms. *Sex Roles, 65*(7/8), 596–605.

Sypeck, M. F., Gray, J. J., Etu, S. F., Ahrens, A. H., Mosimann, J. E., & Wiseman, C. V. (2006). Cultural representations of thinness in women, redux: *Playboy* magazine's depiction of beauty from 1979 to 1999. *Body Image, 3*(3), 229–235.

Tannen, D. (1990). *You just don't understand: Women and men in conversation.* London: Virago.

Tavris, C. (1993). The mismeasure of woman. *Feminism & Psychology, 3*(2), 149–168.

Thompson, L. (2017). Mainstreaming 'Women' without feminisms in psychology. *Social and Personality Psychology Compass, 11*(11), e12359. Available at: https://doi.org/10.1111/spc3.12359.

Thorne, S. R., Hegarty, P., & Hepper, E. G. (2019). Equality in theory: From a heteronormative to an inclusive psychology of romantic love. *Theory & Psychology, 29*(2), 240–257.

Tomasetto, C., Alparone, F. R., & Cadinu, M. (2011). Girls' math performance under stereotype threat: The moderating role of mothers' gender stereotypes. *Developmental Psychology, 47*(4), 943–949.

Townsend, J. M., & Wasserman, T. (1998). Sexual attractiveness: Sex differences in assessment and criteria. *Evolution and Human Behavior, 19*(3), 171–191.

Tuhiwai Smith, L. (2013). *Decolonizing methodologies: Research and indigenous peoples.* London: Zed Books.

Turnbull, B., Graham, M. L., & Taket, A. R. (2017). Pronatalism and social exclusion in Australian society: Experiences of women in their reproductive years with no children. *Gender Issues, 34*(4), 333–354.

Turner, J.S., & Rubinson, L. (1993) *Contemporary human sexuality.* Englewood Cliffs, NJ: Prentice-Hall.

Unger, R. K. (1979). Toward a redefinition of sex and gender. *American Psychologist, 34*(11), 1085–1094.

University and College Union (UCU) (2012). *The position of women and BME staff in professorial roles in UK HEIs*. Available at: https://www.ucu.org.uk/media/5559/ Report-The-position-of-women-and-BME-staff-in-professorial-roles-in-UK-HEIs/pdf/ The_position_of_women_and_BME_staff_in_professorial_roles_in_UK_HEIs.pdf.

Upton, R. L., & Han, S. S. (2003). Maternity and its discontents: 'Getting the body back' after pregnancy. *Journal of Contemporary Ethnography, 32*(6), 670–692.

United States Census Bureau (2017, May). *U.S. Census Bureau's Current Population Survey's fertility supplement*. Available at: https://www.census.gov/newsroom/ blogs/random-samplings/2017/05/childlessness_rises.html.

Vandello, J. A., Bosson, J. K., Cohen, D., Burnaford, R. M., & Weaver, J. R. (2008). Precarious manhood. *Journal of Personality and Social Psychology, 95*(6), 1325–1339.

Vandermassen, G. (2011). Evolution and rape: A feminist Darwinian perspective. *Sex Roles, 64*(9/10), 732–747.

Verniers, C. (2020). Behind the maternal wall: The hidden backlash toward childfree working women. *Journal of Theoretical Social Psychology, 4*(3), 107–124.

Vickers, J. M. (1982). Memoirs of an ontological exile: The methodological rebellions of feminist research, in A. Miles and G. Finn (eds.) *Feminism in Canada: From pressure to politics* (pp. 27–46). Montreal: Black Rose.

Viki, G. T., Abrams, D., & Hutchison, P. (2003). The 'true' romantic: Benevolent sexism and paternalistic chivalry. *Sex Roles, 49*(9), 533–537.

Weisberg, D. S., Keil, F. C., Goodstein, J., Rawson, E., & Gray, J. R. (2008). The seductive allure of neuroscience explanations. *Journal of Cognitive Neuroscience, 20*(3), 470–477.

Weisstein, N. (1973). Psychology constructs the female, in A. Koedt, E. Levine, & A. Rapone (eds.) *Radical Feminism* (pp. 178–197). New York: Quadrangle.

West, C. D., & Zimmerman, D. H. (1977). Women's place in everyday talk: Reflections on parent–child interaction. *Social Problems, 24*(5), 521–529.

West, C., & Zimmerman, D. H. (1987). Doing gender. *Gender & Society, 1*(2), 125–151.

Westmarland, N. (2015). *Violence against women: Criminological perspectives on men's violences*. Abingdon: Routledge.

Wetherell, M. (1995). Romantic discourse and feminist analysis: Interrogating investment, power and desire, in S. Wilkinson & C. Kitzinger (eds.) *Feminism and discourse: Psychological perspectives* (pp. 128–144). London: Sage.

Wetherell, M., & Maybin, J. (1996). The distributed self: A social constructionist perspective, in R. Stevens (ed.) *Understanding the self* (pp. 219–279). London: Sage.

Whitaker, K., & Guest, O. (2020). #bropenscience is broken science: Kirstie Whitaker and Olivia Guest ask how open 'open science' really is. *The Psychologist, 33*, 34–37. Available at: https://thepsychologist.bps.org.uk/volume-33/november-2020/ bropenscience-broken-science.

Wigginton, B., & Lafrance, M. N. (2019). Learning critical feminist research: A brief introduction to feminist epistemologies and methodologies. *Feminism & Psychology*. Available at: https://doi.org/10.1177/0959353519866058.

Wilkinson, S. (1988). The role of reflexivity in feminist psychology. *Women's Studies International Forum, 11*(5), 493–502.

Wilkinson, S., 'aided and abetted by', Condor, S., Griffin, C., Wetherell, M., & Williams, J. (1991) *Feminism & Psychology:* From critique to reconstruction. *Feminism & Psychology, 1*(1): 5–18.

Wilkinson, S. (ed.) (1996). *Feminist social psychologies*. Buckingham: Open University Press.

Wilkinson, S., & Kitzinger, C. (eds.) (1996). *Representing the other: A feminism & psychology reader*. London: Sage.

Williams, J. E., & Best, D. L. (1990). *Measuring sex stereotypes: A multination study.* London: Sage.

Willig, C. (2017). Reflections on the use of object elicitation. *Qualitative Psychology, 4*(3), 211–222.

Wilton, T. (1992). Sisterhood in the service of patriarchy: Heterosexual women's friendships and male power. *Feminism & Psychology, 2*(3), 506–509.

Winn, L., & Cornelius, R. (2020). Self-objectification and cognitive performance: A systematic review of the literature. *Frontiers in Psychology, 11*, 20. Available at: https://doi.org/10.3389/fpsyg.2020.00020.

Wood, R. (2016). 'You do act differently when you're in it': Lingerie and femininity. *Journal of Gender Studies, 25*(1), 10–23.

Wood, W. and Eagly, A. H. (2002). A cross-cultural analysis of the behavior of women and men: Implications for the origins of sex differences. *Psychological Bulletin, 128*(5): 699–727.

World Health Organization (WHO) (2016). *Maternal mental health.* Geneva: WHO.

Wuest, J. (2001). Precarious ordering: Toward a formal theory of women's caring. *Health Care for Women International, 22*(1/2), 167–193.

Yoder, J. D., & Schleicher, T. L. (1996). Undergraduates regard deviation from occupational gender stereotypes as costly for women. *Sex Roles, 34*(3), 171–188.

Yoder, J. D., Tobias, A., & Snell, A. F. (2011). When declaring 'I am a feminist' matters: Labeling is linked to activism. *Sex Roles, 64*(1/2), 9–18.

Young, J. L., & Hegarty, P. (2019). Reasonable men: Sexual harassment and norms of conduct in social psychology. *Feminism & Psychology, 29*(4), 453–474.

Zaslow, E. (2009). *Feminism, Inc.: Coming of age in girl power media culture.* Dordrecht: Springer.

Zimmerman, D. H., & West, C. (1975). Sex roles, interruptions and silences in conversation, in B. Thorne & N. Henley (eds.) Language and sex: Difference and dominance (pp. 105-129). Rowley, MA: Newbury House.

Zukas, M. (1993). Friendship as oral history: A feminist psychologist's view. *Oral History, 21*(2), 73–79.

Index